CLOWNERY

In lieu of a life spent in harness

Paul Hunter

Davila Art & Books

Sisters, Oregon

Publisher: Davila Art & Books LLC.
PO Box 1627 Sisters, Oregon 97759

First Edition January 2017

ISBN 978-1-885210-22-7

*Extravagant thanks are due to the editors of the following publications, where some
of these pieces first appeared, often in slightly different forms:*

*The Raven Chronicles: Vol. 19: A Month Into School, The Little Clown in Seventh
Grade, The Bus Driver Clown*

*Vol. 20: By All Rights the Clown's Soundtrack, Then There was Music and Motion,
And What Was Music Anyhow?*

*Vol. 21: He Was Trying to Recall, He Wondered At and Savored, Hardest Was
Finding a Way Into, But Then He Discovered Some of Those, A Sense of Humor
Was the Sine Qua Non, There Was a Savage Humor Too, Thereby the Clown Grew
Definite, Playful Yet Serious*

*Clover, Volume 6: The Clown Family Moved Into, The Highschool Clown's Hand-
writing, The Old Clown on the Road*

*Volume 12: This Young Man Had a Favorite Uncle, It Was Good He Had All Fred's
Equipment, Sorry Fred His Uncle Did Some Tricks, He Knew Wearing His Uncle's
Fright Wig*

*Small Farmer's Journal, Volume 39, No. 1: There Were Roads to Nowhere, Going
To and Fro Over the Earth*

*Cover art—dressing room and ghost light on Falls Theatre mainstage—
thanks to Kurt Beattie & ACT Theatre, who offered the clown a backstage
peek*

Clownery

Clown: 'clod, clot, lump' in Old Frisian, Dutch.
    1. A countryman, rustic, or peasant. 1563 –O.E.D.

-ery *suffix*. 1. A place for: **bakery**. 2. A collection or class: ***finery***. 3. A state or condition: ***slavery***. 4. Act; practice: ***bribery***. 5. Characteristics or qualities of: ***snobbery***. [Middle English *-erie* from Old French *-er* agent suffix.] –American Heritage Dictionary

Contents

baby clown

"Every man is a divinity in disguise, a god playing a clown."
–Ralph Waldo Emerson

THERE CAME AN ENDLESS SQUEEZE, a shudder then another, a surge and gush, then all at once the gurgle and slurp quieted, the world got busy and bright. What a show! Out of the tunnel these big creatures hovered and swooped, making loud sounds from wide wobbly holes in their faces. The baby clown just wanted to lie back and shut the shutters he didn't know how to work. And find something to suck.

THEY HADN'T BOUGHT A BED YET when they brought him home. So they emptied out a dresser drawer, folded towels to lay him in. There was no hurry, he couldn't peek over the side, wouldn't turn turtle, much less crawl for a while. But whatever visited him seized his whole attention. Hopeful or hopeless, it was all outside him and beyond. A grasping, flailing, floppy mite who practiced making dreamy faces, a wrinkled ancient whose needs were simple: sleep and milk, more sleep and more milk, fresh diapers, moments of outrage, a little cooing and burbling, nothing loud or shiny, cold or hot.

HE DIDN'T YET KNOW WHAT HE WAS, what any of this meant. He hardly knew how to cry, though he must have cried that first time at the outrage being spanked. He beamed at whatever he turned to, whatever moved in the light. When that turned out to be a person, a chuckle would escape him, so quickly he learned to laugh. He put his toes in his mouth for the squirmy taste of them. Everything that moved brought a grab and giggle. When he started to nurse and was suddenly filled up, that called for a mighty burp. When they changed his dirty diapers, he peed straight up in the air. The big ones laughed so hard when he laughed, jumped when he cried, made faces and silly sounds at him, held him over their hearts, where that thumping deep down let him feel safe and sleep tight.

THE BABY CLOWN WAS TEETHING, so cranky and feverish nothing gave him or his folks a moment's rest. His dad was so exhausted he was ready to leave him on the church steps where they'd gotten hitched. His mom wanted to drop him off at the hospital where they'd met. They couldn't think what to do—the orphanages were all locked, their doctor didn't answer his phone after six, and the grandmas lived too far off to make house calls. So they walked to a little corner grocery open late, got him ice cream to play with, went home and let him at it, then cleaned him off and collapsed in a heap.

HIS RAILROAD YARDMASTER GRANDFATHER smelled like a chimney, and wore a big gold watch to help him regulate trains, with a buttery gold fob engraved with his initials on a chain. The only time the teething baby sat in the old man's lap he reached up and bit down on the fob. Forever after the old man carried his sharp little tooth-marks like a stamp of approval. Babies weren't exactly his line, but here was proof how close they could get, how fiercely they hung on.

HE HAD NO CLUE what all these noises meant. Some splashed over him from the big ones leaning down, and some came burbling out of him. Some places also had excitable furry ones underfoot, meowing and barking. All he could do was listen, mimic what he heard and toss it back. It was like playing pinball—sometimes his tongue dropped down a hole and the world lit up. There came a moment when he sensed there had to be more to the game, so got careful imitating what he heard, and was rewarded with caresses, cooing, smiles. Then a ways further on, the notion came on the wing that each of these sounds meant one thing, nothing else, that this babble was one grand, impossible plaything, where sounds flapping on their clothesline meant the world.

AND QUICKLY HE LEARNED ABOUT FALLING. From the time he pulled himself up to chew the rail of his playpen with his sharp new teeth he had the lumps to prove it. He learned how walking was falling you aimed at what drew you, what you craved. And like a romantic he fell for everything. That was the plan anyhow, teeter-tottering along on the level, till he hit a downslope, started windmilling, plunked himself down on his padded tailend for a slide.

HIS DAD WAS STUDYING Pavlovian conditioning when he was born, and all at once here was the perfect guinea pig. As soon as he could stand up in his crib, the dad punched a hole in the top edge of a tin can and tied it to the top rail with a string. Then several times a night he would stand the little clown up, pour water into the can, pull out his penis, stick it in the can and shake it. Soon the sound of running splashing water would make him pee good as Pavlov's other dog, and he quit wearing diapers. But then he would also jump up to pee when he heard rain on the roof.

EVERY BABY WAS A CLOWN, an innocent bumpkin all floppy actions and sounds but no words, as every small child off and on was a huffing little engine that ran loud and silent, hot and cold. By turns fragile and impervious, he could drag a huge adult through a market at breakneck speed, only to collapse in tears when what he wanted wasn't right there anymore. Every drunk aspired to be a baby clown, who could take a fall and bounce up laughing.

THE NAVAJO PEOPLE HAD A CUSTOM of celebrating the first time the new baby laughed. Sometime in the child's first year, whoever could make the baby laugh—and no fair tickling—got to host and pay for a huge party. And there was plenty of competition for the honor. They believed you couldn't have too many family and friends to see you through hard times, so everyone was invited, and told stories of other babies' first laughs. Then the grownups received token gifts of sweets and salt from the baby. For the tiny helpless guest of honor, this was welcome to the human world, at least its amusements and joys.

BEFORE CAR SEATS AND SEAT BELTS his dad let the tiny clown drive. He couldn't see over the wheel unless he stood up. Couldn't reach the pedals anyhow. So he took the top of the wheel while his dad worked the rest, tried to hold it straight as they rumbled along this country road in the balmy air, every now and then tooting the horn at whatever caught his attention, at farmers and corn rows and cows, at chickens and buzzards and clouds.

little clown

"I am too childish-foolish for this world."
–William Shakespeare, Richard III

HIS MOM TOOK HER TWO LITTLE CLOWNS HOME for the duration, as they called it. For the rationing of meat and butter, rubber and gas and shoe leather. For the victory garden worked by grandparents, overgrown as ever. Home to her sister who also had a little boy with a father overseas. Home to nights around the radio, everyone hungry for news from halfway round the world. Home to the outhouse and old farmers clomping into the general store to get their mail and talk over the latest. Farmers who used the wrought-iron boot scraper by the door, the rockers and benches on the porch, the shiny brass spittoons. He was scratching frost flowers off the inside of a kitchen windowpane when he saw his dad dressed all in brown climb down off a bus into a snowdrift and shoulder his duffel bag. Then one of the watchers and waiters behind him said Now there is something to celebrate.

ONE OLD BACHELOR FARMER GAVE the young mother his meat rations to fatten her two little clowns. He kept a coupon or two, he said just enough to make gravy, to pour on pancakes and cornflakes.

EVERY DOOR IN THE HOME PLACE had a doorstop. The floors were uneven in the store and the house built on behind with no front door of its own, which all sat on limestone blocks on the ground where things never finished settling, where summer breezes blew through and teacups in the china cabinet rattled should a grownup take a step. So there was a painted plaster frog and a bearded troll and a goldfish with a gaping mouth, a toy tin truck and a giant south sea shell, heavy things that stood guard year-round by the doors they held open in fine weather. But the most common of all were heavy irons shaped like double-ended boats, set on the wood stove to heat to press clothes, with a coiled spring handle that kept cool, that fit them all.

THEY HAD ICE CREAM PARLOR CHAIRS in the kitchen with coiled steel backs that were unbreakable, though the round wooden seats sometimes got replaced, and a little smokehouse that smelled like a fireplace with chunks of meat hung in its rafters, links of sausage, slabs of bacon and hams, and an alley outside between it and the woodshed where men and boys would pee against the mossy wall, when the outhouse nearby was busy.

THE BIRDS ON A WIRE behind his grandparents' store were his first. Along the gravel road of old State Route 1 the phone lines would hum and crackle as sparrows and starlings clamped their toes on the wire, swaying in the chill wind like musical notes on a staff, spaced out or crowded together. Next spring he would watch them fluff and preen, see where they nested and launched themselves from under the eaves of outbuildings, see them hunt bugs in the yard, pull worms from the plowed lumpy garden. But for now they were strung on a wire, noisy but simplified, way out of reach overhead. He would study them with his mouth open wide as any baby bird's.

WHEN HE FIRST CAME AWAKE, his parents were in the grip of something larger than themselves—the press of duty in a world at war. He watched his mother write letters in blue fountain-pen ink on pale blue airmail sheets that smelled of lilac, and his father's flimsy pages in return, that smelled of tobacco, damp leather and canvas, what old folks round the stove called jungle rot. He watched her make arcing strokes so linked and regular on the unlined sheets, ran his little finger over her parade of loops like a twisty fence, not knowing what they said or meant, and saw how his father's pages came back with heavier darker strokes, between them fencing things that otherwise roamed silent half a world apart.

BUT PAST THE WAR IT TOOK YEARS for his mom and dad to get back together. Even writing letters of longing on flimsy blue paper back and forth, they'd become strangers, grown apart. Some of their friends had it worse, had been apart five years or more, had suffered unspeakable losses. Their generation had found each other as noble, scared girls and boys, and met on the troops' return as tired, wary women and men. It didn't much help when his father walked in, took his first look at the clown's baby brother, and said "Who belongs to this bowlegged rascal?"

WHERE HE WOKE THEY STILL DELIVERED ice in great blocks, carried in by men with tongs and gloves and a quilted pad on one shoulder. There were still thundering coal chutes, the chuff and scrape of coal shovels, the oily dead vegetable feel of coal in the back of the throat. There were horse-drawn milk wagons where the horse knew the route, would stop and go down the street while the milkman took shortcuts through hedges. It was a quieter world that moved at a slower pace, but with no fewer sleepwalkers. Where everyone else had an eye on your business, and might gossip if they chose. Where drip by drip everything changed, the country retreating ever further as farmers cashed in on the boom and along back roads new houses sprang up, then bunches all stuck together, developments. Still in city and country there were pockets the bulldozers overlooked, eddies just to one side of the huge gaudy flow choked with trash, where folks might keep a donkey in the yard, tend a garden, raise red chickens and a billy goat.

THE TINY CLOWN GOT SICK at eighteen months, while Dad was still gone overseas, and Mom was scared of pneumonia, so checked him into a hospital. On the Children's Ward he was a model patient, potty-trained already, curious, not too talkative, polite. It was Christmas time, and one nurse who enjoyed playing with him on her shift taught him The Night Before Christmas. And long after he'd forgotten most of the hospital stay, even the face and name of the nurse who had liked him, he still had the poem letter-perfect, a ghostly presence that must have caught some of her in there—in the litany of reindeer names, the moon on the breast of the new-fallen snow, the cap and kerchief and long winter's nap, the prancing and pawing of each little hoof.

THE TINY CLOWN WAS REACHING UP to show Mom what he had, a plastic comb. She was at the small four-burner gas stove in the basement apartment cooking supper, and the comb had barely touched the burner when it burst into flames. She knocked it out of his wailing grip, snatched him up and skipped to the fridge in one motion. The next thing he knew she was soothing his hand with a cool stick of butter. She asked if he wanted to taste it and he did. Soon they were giggling over his buttery red fingers, and she could turn back to see what else might have burned.

HIS PARENTS TOOK THE LITTLE CLOWN to his first circus, where the real show was the sideshow, not so noisy, and up-close. There was a lady braiding her long beard, and a tattooed man who had scribbled all over himself with colored inks, even behind his ears, between his fingers and toes. And a man with no arms who sat in a crooked highchair, who made his bare feet work like hands. Took out papers and makings, rolled a cigarette that he lit with a pack of matches. Reached up and took his wallet out of his shirt pocket, took out a dollar bill, folded it four times into a tight little square, unfolded it, put it away. But the greatest thing was the elephant. His parents gave him a peanut to feed it, showed him how to hold his hand out flat. But it wasn't like feeding a donkey that could bite. Here the elephant stood bigger than the tent, practically big as the sky, and reached down with her nose like a leather fire hose with hairs and a lip on the end of it, that snuffled at him and his hand, then curled its lip and plucked the peanut, took it all the way up to her mouth. And while the little clown watched, this great wrinkly thing flapped its ears, and with one huge dark eye watched him back. They were standing behind a rope, and the elephant had a chain around one ankle, that went to a truck axle pounded through sawdust down into the dirt. But that was nothing. The elephant could just walk off, and his parents and everyone else here were helpless as he was to stop it. So while he shook with fear and wonder, he fed it more peanuts.

ONE SUMMER SUNDAY MORNING the two tiny clowns found themselves stuck in jail. Their parents had been out partying the night before, and were dead to the world. Since they couldn't escape their cribs, the clowns scooched them over to the open window, and started tossing things out—their blankets and pillows and toys, even their favorite stuffed koala bear. Out this second floor window the things just disappeared, left their world empty and clean. So they took off their pajamas and tossed them out too. Soon there was nothing upstairs but two tiny naked skinny wiggling giggling clowns. All the stuff fluttered down onto bushes in the yard, which finally drew a sober sharp-eyed neighbor to knock on their door and wake the drowsy ogres from their den.

HE WAS WATCHING HIS DAD DRAW a horse. They sat at the kitchen table late Sunday morning after church. This horse was the only thing his dad liked to draw, the one thing he gave himself up to completely, took his time, got into every detail. And always drew the same one. The little clown could almost feel the velvety nostrils and lips quiver under the soft pencil, the teeth chomp, the twitchy ears swivel in all directions, that showed both the horse's mood and what it was listening to. Each muscle of the neck and chest and legs. The hooves that were heavy and light. The still pool of the dark liquid eye. The little clown had a hobby horse with the exact same head nailed to its broomstick, the same nose and chin, the same fine eyelashes. Though it appeared under the Christmas tree with other presents from Santa, he could tell where it was from if he just thought a minute. It was the one thing his father seemed to love enough to look at that long and that close, that he would share.

NEXT TO HIS DAD'S DRAWINGS his own were scratches. His horse was a potato that grew a long nose and a saddle like warts. He'd carve a bridle onto its head like a cage. His pencil couldn't yet speckle the horse's tongue, shade the cheeks and fetlocks and knees, couldn't comb the mane or fluff the tail. It's like his dad's pencil was touching an invisible horse ever so lightly, that the touches would slowly make visible. His dad never drew bridle or saddle or harness, his horse ran free. But was it even a real horse? It was the horse he kept stabled in his mind, knew and cared for, went to over and over, that but for his drawings nobody else got to see.

ONE DAY THE LITTLE CLOWN TAGGED ALONG behind his mother, being a big help toting packages while she shopped. He followed her into the butcher shop for some baloney and salami. There he noticed how closely she studied the butcher, and when they left the shop he asked what she was watching for. She said the butcher's thumb. She said That was how you got cheated, he'd sneak his thumb on the scale when you weren't looking, while he was weighing whatever you bought. Only you wouldn't get to take it home and cook it up, this imaginary half-pound that vanished just like that. That went away like your lap when you stood up.

HE HAD JUST SAT UP IN THE BACK SEAT, his brother near him asleep on a blanket. They were driving nonstop to California, whatever that was. Wherever he woke up was somewhere else, his parents in the front seat quietly talking, his dad driving, smelling of coffee and cigarettes, with only the whistle of a wind-wing cracked. Here was nothing but water, a narrow two-lane road floating on muddy water alongside and all around as far as he could see. There was mist on the water, once in a while the roof of a house or barn, but no cows, no birds, no boats, no trees. There was also no room to pull off or turn around, no way to do anything but what they did, drive on top of the water on into the emptiness, though his parents stayed calm.

IN THE MOUNTAINS THEY ROUNDED A BEND and the car was swallowed by a dusty sea of cows. Thousands and millions bawling, swinging their horns and tails, stirring clouds that turned the sun red. There were a few cowboys on horses, real cowboys with bandannas over their noses, and some with city-man hats, with no boots and no guns. There wasn't much they could do but swing their ropes and whistle. The cows went their ways in no hurry, passing for over an hour through and around the cars stuck there. Nobody honked or yelled anything. When they rolled the windows down on account of the heat, the cow smell blew in so fresh they rolled them back up again.

THEN THEY WERE HIGH IN A MOUNTAIN PASS where his dad pulled over and jumped out. Dad said Think of that, still summer and it's winter here. Mom said Let's go, it's getting cold. Dad handed each of the little clowns a snowball to eat, and they did, though it tasted dusty and dry, not like much of anything. Dad said I wanted to stop at Pike's Peak, but this is almost as good. They'll remember this all their lives.

THE TINY CLOWN RAN UP TO HIS MAMA on the beach, said Mama, we cooking. And there on a flat rock it was. They had wet sand patties, hamburgers, fish sticks, biscuits, cookies—that they were carefully turning with a shingle they'd found up the beach, to do the other side. Yum, she said, and in a few minutes was served dinner on another scrap of wood, solemnly told if she ate it all she'd get dessert, so she did. They were deeply amused watching her work two twigs for chopsticks, how she actually ate some real seaweed. Then the cooks stirred up strawberry ice cream in their bucket, which Mom said tasted salty but perfect.

ON THE RUG THE TOY TRAIN hopped off the tracks. Dishes rattled in the hutch but nothing broke. The little house creaked like a ship, shook and shook. Mom sat waiting for it to be over, saying nothing, like she was praying or being polite. Then she said that was an earthquake. She didn't seem to much like it, but wasn't too upset. The little clowns wondered if the ground could open up and swallow them, but knew better than ask any grownup.

HIS NEXT TIME AT THE OCEAN playing in the surf the tiny clown got knocked down by a wave. He bounced up wailing and sputtering at the injustice. He would feel the sting in his eyes, up his nose, taste the salt grit in his mouth all his days. For years after it took work to get him near big water, work to learn to swim and overcome what yanked him off his feet and shoved him under, mollify that sudden biting fear. But then one day he was a dogfish, all four paws paddling while his snout blew bubbles, and the water was friendly once more. Still, he knew better than to turn his back on its endless moody games, how it sparkled and pranced, how it stormed in and skittered away.

HE SAW A NEWSREEL OF PRESIDENT Harry Truman eating his straw hat in a big bowl of milk, because he'd lost a bet. At least that's who he thought it was. His mom said that the hat was specially made out of shredded wheat. He thought it was a good idea to wear something edible for when you got hungry or lost a bet, and paid attention ever after to food disguises. A gun made of licorice. Big red wax lips. Edible underwear. Decades later Pat Paulson would appear—a presidential candidate who invented shoes made out of the skin on chocolate pudding.

HE CAME RUNNING IN FROM PLAYING in the yard, hugged his mother and told her he loved her. She studied him, said what for? He turned it over in his head in slow-motion like a melting ice cream cone, licked every reason he could think of. Could there be just one? Together they were overwhelming, like a box of crickets, each chirping its own song, a commotion that all came out as one. Here he was, pure impulse, stuck in his tracks, captured by a look. Why did he love her? 'Cause you cook good, he said, and raced off.

THE LITTLE CLOWN FELT MOMENTARY even to himself—
flighty, transitional, of two minds at each crossing, one slow to catch on
dawdling like a possum, one leaping unpredictable as a deer in the head-
lights. So by quick turns he'd feel confused and calm, frightened and
fearless, lost knowing right where he'd been just a heartbeat ago. Every
new aha plucked away dirty goggles, but dealt him fresh delusions as he
rubbed sleep from his eyes. For a while he'd tell himself Oh, so that's it,
now I get it, twenty times a day, while his kangaroo mind always kept
one jump ahead.

SERIOUS ABOUT EVERY LITTLE THING, still his mind would
romp and soar. One morning after hearing the story of the grasshopper
and the ants, he suspected he was more of a guilty grasshopper who'd
fiddle and watch others work, so he went out to find some ants and see
for himself. Flopping down in the grass, he soon saw he couldn't tell
the first thing about them. Never mind age or identity, were they girls
or boys? He couldn't tell if they ever slept or took time off from their
endless foraging. When they met they rubbed each others' feelers, but
what did that mean? Could they see in the dark, or did they have to feel
their way? Their world seemed all eating and fighting and taking care of
the nest—but were they dumb or smart? From up here a foot away they
seemed busy and serious, each with a job and a path. But could their
whole little lives be a joke?

THE LITTLE CLOWN WAS SPANKED with a slipper, with an egg-
turner, a hair brush, with whatever came to hand, even the bare hand
itself that stung the worst and drew a wince of pain from the angry par-
ent. He didn't much like it but that was supposed to be the point. His
little brother clown just laughed. So corrections never worked as intend-
ed. They made him sullen and rebellious, with drooping tail feathers still
smarting from the well-earned wallop. But somewhere along in there
he saw he got to choose his mood, that the big ones were right, he was
wrong. That defiant laughter didn't work. You caught more flies with
honey than vinegar. It was the guilty gotcha he needed to get past.

AT ONE POINT HE CRAVED the authority and continuity of
church, its secret shadows, sounds and scents. Where people came to sit

quiet, admit they felt lost, wait for answers. Where the voices of men and women rose in song to the rafters, with their echoes tried to fill the silence overhead. Where messages for today were selected and explained out of the big old book of contradictions, picking through its anger and vengeance to unearth its blinding lights. Where the little clown felt guilty because he did some of his best thinking in the lulls between priest and ceiling fan droning on in their forgotten tongues, that let him think things on the wing, or nod off at least and find rest.

RIDING IN THE BACK SEAT TO INDIANA one hot summer Saturday morning, a whole story appeared in a flash: a wedding at a little country church outside Harrison, its big fancy car waiting decorated with a tail of tin cans, shaving cream windows, strings of balloons. It was the only show in town, with everyone inside, organ music and singing coming out the open doors. Just then around the church came a baby horse left out of the party that had gotten loose, that teetered up the front steps on its long legs for a peek, that a lady in a long dress ran to catch.

ON THE FARM HE WAS FOLLOWING his uncle Edwin at a distance, up from the lower pasture. Edwin was carrying the newborn calf cradled in burlap, with the mother right on his heels. The baby was still damp. She'd licked it off, but it couldn't yet stand or walk. Mom was intent but exhausted, moving slowly, stumbling, huffing in the chilly air, and didn't want any little clowns around. Any time he got too close she would turn on him, lower her head to run him off. This wasn't her first, so she mostly surrendered to Edwin's calm and quiet. But if the baby made a sound she'd bawl in answer, and lean in to see what was what. And he'd stop for as long as she wanted, since for now she was boss.

WHEN EDWIN'S DRAFT HORSES WERE WORKING they crowded out all the little clown's cowboy thoughts. When they pranced and romped they shook the earth. Superior beings, everything about them astonishing, how tall and wide awake they were, how curious and observant, how far they reached those long necks for what they ate, how delicately and voraciously they drank from the trough, how they pooped while walking, raised their tails and let fly, thought nothing of it. Any-

21

thing behind them was past, unless they were hitched to it and pulling. Though they stood obedient as monuments, theirs was life undeniable, all but absolute. Whenever there was a pause they reached for a bite of what offered. When things hitched behind them got quiet, their long heads swung around for a look.

UNCLE EDWIN HAD A BOAR the size of a pony, with tusks like can-openers. With glittering mad little eyes no telling what he thought. He filled the stake-sided pickup when they loaded him to take to some neighbor's place to, as Edwin said, introduce him to their ladies. They didn't have to warn the little clown not to pet him, to stay clear. The only thing they had more dangerous was the dairy bull who wouldn't fit in the pickup and needed a six-stranded smooth wire fence taller than he was to hold him, that he would slam into sometimes just so folks could feel it bulge and groan, remind them what was barely contained there, kept waiting.

GROWNUPS ALWAYS HAD SOMETHING TO DO, though few kids wanted to watch old guys straighten a coffee can of bent nails on an anvil, to make storm repairs. On such days the clown learned to make do and save scraps, use what was handy right now to stop rain blowing sideways into the barn or hen house.

HE SAW HOW FARMING GAVE YOU something different to do every day. And doing it a little at a time kept your footing, kept you moving, whether it was a hundred feet of new fence, or an acre to be cleared of brambles and thistles. There were rushes with planting and harvesting, getting crops and livestock to market, but then there were also days with the fence done and the brush cut to where you could go fishing, or sit and watch chickens compare notes as they scratched out a living, study how cows kept clear of each another, eating their ways up a hillside.

THE LITTLE CLOWN LOVED WATCHING hand-cranked silent movies on the farm, on a sheet pinned up to the parlor wall. How jerky the motions, oddly cocky, fearless and abrupt. What they loved were cartoons and comedies, Keaton and Chaplin and Felix the Cat. They had little patience with melodrama, would tear though it at breakneck speed that could make anything funny. Like the other little ones he itched to crank it himself, to control the pace—slow it down, speed it up, wind it backwards. There was that steady clicking sound as you cranked—and how the focus kept slipping, that you had to readjust. And then, if it got stuck, the image would smoke and burn till all you had left was an atom bomb, a white-hot steady light.

BEING THE BIG FROG IN A SMALL POND mattered to some more than others. You needed to be where there were things to eat, where not so many might eat you. If you liked being boss it was nice to have your own pond out of the way of bigger frogs. But if you were a little frog, what did it even matter? Hanging out at the top of the stairs, he overheard the big people at the party below argue this point in loud laughing voices, and as he drifted off he thought of night sounds around ponds, the plunk of a few loud deep voices, then a pause, then the rest would join in a nattering chorus, then settle back, drink in the night a beat, then a deep plunk start again.

LITTLE PITCHERS HAVE BIG EARS, the folks would say around the little clown listening intently to their talk of big-people things. He knew he had big ears. But pitchers also had a fat lip and a handle. And baseballs he pitched hard but crooked. So he thought he caught their signal, but couldn't see what was so funny about an aunt's time of month, what that had to do with her shouting at an uncle jailed for drunken monkeyshines. Who even knew what a monkeyshine was?

HE THOUGHT HIS EARS STUCK OUT, and they did—he looked like he was flying. How come all these big people got nice flat ears they could tuck pencils behind, and run faster than the wind? Then one day his father explained they got nice and flat when you put the fifteen pound weight of your head on them to sleep. So for a while he wondered was he resting evenly, heaving his big-headed skinny self from side to side. Then he noticed that big ears had another use. They kept your head from rolling off the pillow, starting a nightmare avalanche.

KIDS WOULD JOKE among themselves about nightly prayers, in bed after lights-out recite, Now I lay me down to sleep, my little old Ford's parked out in the street. If I should die before I wake, I pray the Lord to pull the brake. They never let grownups hear this, though it didn't seem such a sacrilege. Folks prayed for odd selfish whims all the time, and knew even serious prayers went unanswered. While cars popped out of gear in the night and rolled away.

IN THE LATE 40s HOSPITALS STILL BELIEVED flowers at night breathed out something harmful for patients, so nurses set vases of cut flowers out in the corridors. Every now and then the clown's resident dad on nightly rounds would steal one flower from each bunch, take home a bedraggled mismatched bouquet for the kitchen table next morning— daisies and tulips, roses and lilies and forget-me-nots, rolled up in a damp newspaper, all one gorgeous riot. It was their little joke. The nurse mom knew right where they came from, though there was never a note.

EVEN AS A PEEWEE HE KNEW BIRDS didn't just sing their names over and over. They had things to tell one another, but were mostly content with the equivalent of Hey you—over here, broadcast to a world that might neither listen nor care. Sometimes it was like wartime radio, where a hawk in an oak might be a spy listening in. But the little birds hid and sung on. He savoured their liquid embellishments—their riffs and filigree, each a silk banner hung on the shimmering air.

THEN THERE CAME SCHOOL. The kindergarten clown was enlisted as a special courier, carrying messages behind enemy lines like a passenger pigeon, footloose, wobbling along with clipped wings. Each little clown in his class was required to have a bag with a permanent loop to go around his neck, with the kid's name permanently sewn on the face of it, that could hold a business envelope, that was closed with a zipper or snaps. This was for communiqués between school and home, report cards signed and returned, forms to be filled out, money for school trips and projects. Though he could already read, he was sworn to abide by the code of the secret agent, and never once opened the bag he wore every Friday and Monday. It made him feel proud, since his mom made such a nice one, stitched his name in cursive red thread, but sometimes he also felt like a prize chump forced to squeal on himself.

ONE WINTER DAY THE TWO LITTLE CLOWNS were out play-
ing in the winter woods, when they found a drainage ditch full of water
frozen over. Deep, way over their heads, and neither one could swim.
The littler one danced out on the rubber ice that squeaked and flexed,
humming a little tune. It was like a waltz on a trampoline, a clear drum-
head he could see black water through, exciting and daring till it splin-
tered and swallowed him. The older clown dragged a fallen sapling over,
pushed it out to him, yelled to hang on, then ran to get their mom. He'd
never seen her move so fast, no coat no hat downstairs across the muddy
yard into woods where she grabbed the branch the little one clung to
and pulled him in hand over hand. Didn't bother to swat him, shout
or whisper, snatched him up, held him tight and shining all wet huff-
ing clouds of steam running back inside, with the bigger clown trailing
behind, his legs shaking, his feet muddy balls so thick he could hardly
move.

THEY WATCHED SOME BIGGER BOYS borrow tools from their
dad, then start digging a big square hole at the edge of the woods behind
where they lived. They watched the sod roll up, the dirt pile grow as the
hole went down, watched the boys gather heavy poles cut from saplings
in the woods to lay across the hole at last deep enough that all but the
tallest could stand up. The boys nailed a ladder to go down, gathered
some crates and baskets to sit on, then covered the poles with a lattice
of branches they wove, and on top of that unrolled the sod, the grass
and weeds they'd started with. It was a hideout, a smoky burrow the
little clowns never got to see inside once the lid was back on, where
everything happened by lamplight and candlelight. Where dark schemes
might be hatched, cards played and jokes told, pilfered beer sipped and
butts puffed, things they hardly dared dream of.

CHEAP ROLLER SKATES WITH A KEY were a royal pain. You
could screw them on so tight they pinched your toes through your shoes
and still they'd work loose and dump you on the sidewalk, skin your el-
bows and knees. The metal wheels made a crashing shushing sound like
a drummer's riff on an ashcan. The idea was kids' feet grew so fast the
skates could be adjusted, worn year after year, passed around, handed

down. But they needed someplace smooth to skate on. Kids in the country couldn't skate on gravel. The little clown's country parents told him how the ice skates they had as kids worked the same way, but stayed on better since your feet turned to blocks of ice. But when they played Crack the Whip, they'd shake the one on the end right out of his shoes.

THAT SPRING THE MOTHER HAD ABOUT HAD IT with them tracking mud in the house from the woods. She'd reminded, pleaded and threatened to no avail. Two sets of muddy tracks still dogged their heels indoors. So today she sat them down, removed their shoes, made them wash their hands and go sit at the kitchen table. Then she solemnly served each a plate with a muddy footprint pried off his own shoe, set on a square of waxed paper, along with a glass of tapwater. The little eyes grew to saucers. There was the silence of the tomb. Mud for lunch. They could hardly look at each other. Their little clown stocking feet hung limp, unable to even touch the floor. Then out of nowhere their chicken noodle peanutbutter and jelly salvation landed, still without a word.

ON A RARE DAY OFF THEIR DAD MADE a big plain kite on the kitchen table, on a cross of sticks, of brown wrapping paper and string. He made it with care, pasted it smooth and flat, knotted a tail of torn rags ten feet long, and off they went on this windy March day, to the top of Eden Park to go fly it. It was stronger than other kites flying that day, thicker skinned, with a longer bushier tail, so flew higher without waggling and diving to earth in the gusts like a devil dragon or bucking bronco. When they ran out of string their dad left them together holding onto the stick at the end and ran to buy more. Three balls of string later the kite still flew, tadpoled to the far side of town miles away, where the string sagged of its own weight and finally broke. They drove to where it had gone down and there it was, caught but still perfect, fluttering in the crown of the tallest tree.

HE HAD AN UNCLE who liked to tickle him hard. Which wasn't funny and it wasn't fair. This uncle, his godfather, had been a bootlegger who drove a Moon roadster through Prohibition, but now was a baker with big strong hands, and at family gatherings he would grab the skinny kid and dig his fingers into him till he couldn't breathe, till he gasped and went limp on the ground. No one ever stopped the uncle from doing this, but the small clown learned to stay away from him, avoid coming within arm's reach, especially when the grownups' voices had grown loud, with a whiff of booze in the air.

HE WONDERED HOW HE COULD BE so ticklish, yet couldn't tickle himself. He sat on the bed one morning and tried hard, but nothing worked. Armpits, ribs and belly, behind his knees, even the soles of his feet. Yet if someone did it to him, he could be tickled till he gasped for air and blacked out. Was it because he couldn't go too far, couldn't help trusting himself?

ONE RAINY DAY THEIR MOM SAID why don't you go down and play in the basement. But the two little clowns said it was dark and scary down there. When their dad came home that night he said let's go have a look. He gave each of them a flashlight and led them down. There was the giant furnace octopus, and the musty smell, but in the shadows there was other stuff. A bin with black dust in the bottom that used to be coal. He pointed out all the plumbing and wiring. Where to turn off the power to the fuse box. Where to shut off the water should they ever spring a leak. He said the basement was where you got to see what made everything work, not hidden away behind walls. Down here you saw the truth.

ONE OF THOSE CHILLY BRIGHT FALL DAYS they brought a box turtle down to the basement to play with, that they had found in the woods. But then it crawled off to some corner and they lost track of it. It would be spring before they were back down there again, and when the turtle crawled out of the shadows, so skinny and dry at first they were ashamed to go near it, like it was some kind of ghost. But then they took heart, carried it out in the yard, and put it down in the bushes, where it scrambled to get away from them.

SNATCHED OUT OF A SOUND SLEEP and paddled hard, it took the little clowns a woolly minute to figure out what they'd done. They had left a tricycle and a wagon behind the car, and their dad called to the hospital in the middle of the night had backed over them. But he was more bent out of shape than their toys were. It didn't make sense right then and didn't later by the sorry light of day. They thought their punishment should be the mangled toys. But something like this must have landed on their dad when he was small, a summary judgment by his own dad who worked the railroad night shift, who never made mistakes even in the dark, and pounced on those who did. Because for both of them mistakes cost lives.

HE DIDN'T WANT TO GET BUNDLED UP to go out and play, because his dad never did. He'd just run out and jump in the car. But in this storm their mother said they would need raincoats and hats and galoshes. So they were standing there all buckled up when their dad ran downstairs, set to leave for work. He asked his dad why he didn't bundle up, and his dad said Because I can run between the raindrops! The two little clowns watched to see if he would get wet as he zigzagged out to the car.

IN THE CLOWN'S NEIGHBORHOOD there was a big plump politician who always wore a classic white clown suit on Halloween, with puffy red buttons down its front the size of cupcakes, with ruffles at his neck and ankles and wrists, with a white hat shaped like a ski slope of ice cream, sporting makeup and lipstick and a big cigar. Like a character in a sobbing clown opera, this old ward boss took charge of the occasion on his block. With the election just around the corner he worked the crowd of parents and kids. Standing under a streetlight he held forth, smoked and joked, amazed folks with his mental juggling, greeting everyone by name, even those who'd never met him, even little ones in the dark seen right through their disguises, shaking hands and laughing, passing out lollipops and candy bars, cigars and business cards.

HE HAD THE PERFECT PIRATE SHIRT for Halloween, short-sleeved with red and blue stripes. It went just right with his pinned-up slouch hat and wooden cutlass and eye patch. But then as the sun set the night turned cold, with frost on the windows and roofs. And he had no pirate coat of blue wool with brass buttons. So despite hot tears of protest, they wouldn't let him go trick-or-treating half naked. And he sat smoldering till his younger brother came home, the burnt cork on his face still showing some hobo. He solemnly poured out his bag of treats on the rug, and like a fellow pirate shared his booty even-steven.

HE KNEW EVEN THEN that hand-puppets were fiercer and lustier than marionettes. Theirs was a disguise for flesh and blood thrust out of the deep underbelly of living, rather than dancing on air, its dainty ways conjured like some kind of fishing lure. Smart aleck Howdy Doody versus lovable Kukla and Ollie. Pulling strings, making the little person dance without muscles or nerves from outside and above felt like playing God, where shoving your fist inside Punch or Judy and working your fingers was crude but strong, and more than a little devilish. Plus it mattered where the voice came from, down from above or up from below. Fran also worked Lambchop, the first sock puppet, its famous face a pucker. Then twenty years later he saw the Muppets, with several people groping around under the table doing who-knew-what to work one jaunty terrycloth person. Probably sitting in each others' laps all tied in knots. His clown mind was totally blown when the fuzzy guy peeled off one eye and stuck it on top of his head.

ONE BROKE CHRISTMAS SANTA BROUGHT them a huge pile of balloon animals and nothing else. Dogs and bears and elephants, horses, cats and bunnies, and a sea-serpent-dragon or dinosaur. Underneath the pile was a note from Santa that said the sled had broken down, and that he'd come back in a couple days. And p.s., thanks for the milk and cookies. So two days after Christmas a big brown Sears truck came to the door, and two men in brown outfits unloaded two big cardboard boxes that said they contained bicycles. When the clowns asked who they were, they said they were Ernie and Bill, Santa's elves, but don't tell anyone. The little clown said If you're elves, how come you're so big? They laughed and said Elves come in all sizes.

LEARNING TO SWIM OR RIDE A BIKE taught the little clown one thing: as soon as you trusted them not to let go they let go. They pretended they couldn't keep up with you drowning and crashing, but that was a laugh. They were giants, all they had to do was reach out their sausage fingers and you were caught. And yet they had to let go, even he knew that. How else would you find out you could float long enough to claw your way though the water, or pedal till the pumping quit making you wobble? But then he noticed they also never said how to stop, like you were born knowing, or had to start out with a crash.

THEIR HEADBOARD BANGING THE WALL woke him. He could hear a couple of his parents' friends there for a visit squeaking in the bed across the hall. He listened hard, heard both of them moaning. It sounded like they were in pain, groaning out a wordless dialogue that only grew louder and fiercer, endless questions and answers that seemed to settle nothing, uproars and outcries that built to a crisis. There was a quiet moment, then murmurs, whispers, soft laughter like rain in the trees. What it was about he couldn't fathom. It sounded like they'd gone to bed with a secret that threatened to kill them, then changed its mind and tried to tell them a joke that was not even funny.

HIS DAD SMEARED POTATOES with wet clay from the crick, then rolled them in the coals as the blaze of the campfire died down. This was a kind of picnic they had never done before, didn't understand this eating out after dark in their own back yard, sitting on damp ground, poking potatoes around, telling stories. Baked beans cooking in their opened tincans, labels burned off, set aside with a pliers to grab the rim. And one shared spoon, he said smiling, like hobos. The grownup memories from that dark time themselves like coals barely glowed through their ash, just don't try to touch one. He told about shooting sparrows to pluck and deepfry, stealing watermelons to cut out the seedless heart, eat the best and leave the rest. Field corn baked in their shucks in the coals just like this. Then the dark lumps of potato were poked, pronounced done. Flipped from the fire, at first playing hot-potato hot-potato hand to hand till one cooled, its baked clay shell cracked and peeled, smeared with butter, sprinkled with salt, at last bit into gingerly, teeth bared. It had a faint burnt taste, in the dark a gritty wonder. Then they all licked off their hands.

HIS DAD SAID THE SCARIEST THING he did in the war was the lifeboat drill, where they spread cargo netting over the bow of the hospital ship and made everybody climb down into the life boats. This included passing down patients strapped to stretchers. If you lost your footing or grip it was a forty foot drop—you hoped you missed anyone or anything below and just hit water. Of course this was the scariest thing when the Zeros weren't shooting at you, aiming at that big red cross on the smokestack.

FOR A YEAR OR TWO EVERY NIGHT their dad would tell them bedtime stories out of Swiss Family Robinson and Tom Sawyer and Huckleberry Finn, but with a difference. His stories always included the two little clowns, who did everything with Tom and Huck and Jim and the Robinsons, painted the fence, got lost in the fog on the river, got swindled by the duke and the dolphin, built a tree house to live in, saw the anaconda crush and swallow the donkey, all that, got thrilled by adventures they already knew would never harm a hair of their sleepy heads.

THE FIRST TIME HE WATCHED its round blizzard face light up, he instantly understood the one saving grace of TV, even as it mesmerized him, made him go limp in its grip. No matter what TV might dish up, it couldn't see you. It was like radio in the dead of night, safe no matter what horrors it dredged up. They didn't know how you took it, what made you shriek and jump, or get bored to tears, or indifferent enough to go make a snack. Whoever sent you this stuff to watch sometimes was like your parents when they'd been out for the evening. Coming home they'd put a hand on the set to see if the dumb thing was still warm. That just gave them one more worry, but said nothing about you.

ONE RAINY SATURDAY HE WATCHED an old black-and-white movie that flickered so bad it seemed to be storming there too. It was about a man locked in a prison where water ran down the walls, where the real punishment came when they forgot all about you, about your crime and sentence, even your real name. Like his father when he was mad, shouting You're grounded forever! Then your hair would grow down past your shoulders, your clothes become smelly rags, the jailor ever fatter as he ate up your food with his own, while you got so skinny you could burrow under dirty straw, dive down a rat hole, worm your way out through a chink in the wall.

ONE MORNING OUT IN THE COUNTRY the little clown's mother was washing her mother's hair in the kitchen pantry, behind the curtain where they boiled their water and took their washtub baths. Postmistress, storekeeper, organist, Grandma always looked serious in her rimless spectacles, wore her long silver-gray hair pinned up in a bun like the weight of the world. But he hadn't known how shiny and beautiful it was. When she came out from behind the curtain in her robe without her glasses, with her skin pink and soft all at once she looked young. Her hair was still damp, and hung down below her waist so far she couldn't sit down. The daughter gently brushed and combed it while she stood and slowly turned like a music box dancer till her shiny tent was dry. Then together they braided and pinned up its silvery coils, tucked away its sparkling magic, so Grandma could sit down and drink her tea, while her daughter stirred oatmeal for the early-bird clown. Forever after, this would be what letting your hair down meant, which in time he would come to understand both as shared love play, and as a sign of release from work, from one's burdens and cares. In this drawing of pins and uncoiling of tresses he saw her slow measured dance as reward.

RUNNING AROUND THE CORNER OF THE BARN he came upon his grandmother on a stool in the shade, plucking a chicken. He hadn't seen her kill it but the ax must have just dropped. She had plunged it in a pot of boiling water nearby that still held a faint bloody ribbon, and was now wrenching out feathers, a tight little bunch at a time. He could see the twist of her grip, hear the little tearing sound as they pulled free. She smiled shyly up at him but said nothing as her hands fiercely undressed the bird. Now to empty out the guts, chop the feet off, cut in parts and toss in the pot, mix up and roll out some dumplings, for a supper that had to taste of this place, its cistern and dirt, blood and gravel, only short stagger-steps from the living.

OUT OF SHAME FOR DISTANT AGGRESSIONS and atrocities they hid parts of themselves from the neighbors, even from the little farm world that was not all German but mostly just like them. To avoid drawing attention to themselves, inviting trouble, they hid parts of themselves even from themselves, and for two world wars became decent plain Americans from nowhere Indiana, without a past, as if there could be such a thing. So it was a rare moment when he heard his grandparents Cecilia and Honus lean into each other and sing Stille Nacht, Heilige Nacht, all six verses in quavering harmonies, while their grown children and little ones held their breath.

IN THE LULL BETWEEN WORLD WARS old folks recalled dancing around the Maypole on a lawn, girls and boys in garlands dancing toward and through one another, weaving colored ribbons in stately skipping steps to the music, over and under out and in, that met at last in a standstill. There they bowed to the one they'd been paired with by chance, let go their ribbons, held hands to continue the dance. The priest considered this a pagan ritual, preferred a chaste procession crowning the statue of the Virgin as Queen of the May. But farmers told of doings in the old country, of May baskets of flowers and treats hung on the doorknob of one's sweetheart in secret the night before May Day, a sweet step beyond valentines.

AT THE END OF FIRST GRADE HE WON the award for best student. It was a pin, a gilt metal banner with the word "winner" engraved on it, and the year on the end of a chain. He'd never known such things existed. He did what he was told, was rarely shushed, but more than that he loved school, loved learning, savored its fearless play and went at it like a rubber buzzsaw. But he also learned new words that final day: kiss-ass and brown-nose. No one bothered explaining envy and sour grapes and the need to get along. He never wore the award. And made sure he never won it again.

IT TOOK A WHILE TO EVEN NOTICE he was ambidextrous. Didn't spot others using a left hand to brush their teeth or comb their hair, or crack an egg in a pan. It was playing baseball where he first saw the southpaw advantage, the batter one step closer to first. But in school he was trained to write and do everything right-handed, though at home he'd done most things left-handed. Maybe the knuckle-rapping nuns who taught him still believed those medieval superstitions, the dexterous and sinister hints of one's handedness. How even ambidextrous meant double-dealing.

THEN WHEN HE WAS SEVEN HE HEARD that Bedouin tribes in the Arabian desert ate with their right hands and wiped their butts with their left. So it was an insult to offer the wrong hand to shake, and seemed enough reason to switch.

HE LEARNED ABOUT SANTA THE HARD WAY in second grade. They were riding in the back seat of the car a few days past Christmas, when his younger brother started arguing with his dad about which presents were his and which were the little clown's. And what Santa had meant by giving him this or that. It was complicated, and his brother felt so aggrieved that he went on and on, spiraling down until his dad lost his temper, glared in the rearview mirror and shouted over his shoulder that he knew what Santa had meant and what Santa wanted because he WAS Santa, he had bought all those presents, and he didn't want to hear another word! And for the rest of the ride in silence they tried to sort out what that meant.

HE FELT FOOLISH TO BE SO EASILY CAUGHT. Last one through the gate coming up from the barn lot for lunch, he'd slipped his little finger through a link of the chain that held it shut, and it wouldn't come back out. There he stood, tugging, stuck. Everybody else was already out of sight. So he tried to free himself. Twisted and pulled but the chain was spiked to the post. Tried to spit on his finger, but his mouth was parched. Called out Hey there, forced himself not to yell Help. Waited some more, then called out Hey a little louder. And again called out. Finally a grownup cousin came looking for him, saw his predicament, said Just stay put, fetched an enamel wash basin with water and a pale sliver of soap, the house kind, not the rough brown kind from out by the cistern pump. Splashed water over his hand then soaped it up, let the swollen knuckle cool and get slippery enough to pop free like a cork. The cousin never said a word to the others, for which he was thankful, though the clown still felt the bump of his joke, Just stay put.

THE FARMERS WERE THRESHING WHEAT on the farm, and the little clowns wanted to see everything while trying to keep out from underfoot. It was all being done the old way, with horses mowing and pulling the binder as it cartwheeled along, then hauling wagonloads of wheat shocks to the threshing machine. Powered by a wide belt running off a tractor parked forty feet away, the tall thing was chittering and squeaking like a shaken cage full of starlings. It had a metal snout that shot a stream of bright yellow straw onto a pile big as it was, and a smaller snout that tumbled the grain into sacks. Every grownup there had a job tending or feeding something, and it was all running full-tilt when the clown's little brother ducked under the moving belt, got snatched and thrown like a puppet off into the weeds. He yelled and all at once everything got quiet. His brother was taken to the hospital, got a nifty airplane brace on his left arm that stayed paralyzed for months, that stuck his arm up and out with a hinge at the elbow. For the rest of that day the farmers told scary stories about how dangerous those belts were, all the hair and pitchforks they'd snatched.

ON A HAYRIDE ONE CHILLY NIGHT under a harvest moon the little clown burrowed down in the loose, fragrant clover and timothy, with them all singing in time to the harness jingle, the team's hollow footfalls and ringing iron rims on the gravel. Uncle Edwin drove looking straight ahead while his daughters with their dates sang and clapped out The stars at night / are big and bright //// Deep in the Heart of Texas, though it could never not be Indiana, staring straight up past clouds into the stars, the bright moon hung like a lantern, his last waking thought Did the night sky sparkle the same everywhere?

young clown

"A clown is like aspirin, only he works twice as fast." –Groucho Marx

BORN IN THE MIDDLE OF WWII the clown was neither a boomer nor buster. Older kids born in the Great Depression told of growing up where half the adults had no work till the war gave everyone a job. Except for farm kids lucky to be fed, many left home early as they could, hopped a freight or stuck out their thumb, looking for work on the bum, not wanting to be a burden. In his schoolyard, in cub scouts then boy scouts, kids played with military gear, camped in pup tents, wore cutoff old uniforms. Some boasted of fathers and uncles and big brothers who landed at Anzio for the drive up the boot, or at Omaha Beach on D-Day, or waded ashore to fight in the jungles of Guadalcanal or the caves on Iwo Jima. Some had never known fathers but for a photo in uniform on the mantel to anchor bedtime prayers, some struggled to even find words for what happened so far away so long ago, without the ghost of a story.

CUTTING THE TREE DOWN WITH HAND-AXES took all day. Their little fingers blistered, their little arms turned to pink putty. They'd clearly picked the wrong tree but once started kept at it, a hard dead sweetgum big around as a fat grownup head, with no bark left and no leaves. After a while they thought to sharpen their little axes with stones and files. Then they went back to chopping on opposite sides like a couple of beavers spitting wood chips. Hours later they moved around and started connecting the two notches. Several times they thought it was getting wobbly, heard cracking sounds and jumped back, but like beavers they only knew to keep going. Finally it was suppertime. Luckily somewhere in the night with nobody watching the tree dropped.

HE COULD BE SURPRISED AT what provoked him, stirred something in him to take charge and settle things. He and his brother might occasionally fight, but that was something else, sparring as practice standing your ground where, should you daydream half a minute, he might snatch your cookie. But one Saturday out behind the garage a bigger kid was hanging out with these two skinny clowns. When they showed him the box turtle they'd found, its bright splashes of yellow and orange like an earthbound butterfly, he picked up a big rock and crushed it. The clown jumped the laughing murderer before he could even straighten up, hung around his neck and pounded him till he ran off and never came back, though the attack was no more bother than a yellowjacket.

THE CLOWNS WERE ALL EXCITED. There in the school yard at recess was a Duncan yo-yo Champion. He wore a jacket that said so, pulled two gold and rhinestone yo-yos out of his pockets already hooked to bandaged middle fingers, and twirled them in the air like six-shooters. He proceeded to do all the famous tricks—some of them mirrored, double, one in each fist. Around the World, Rock the Baby, Loop the Loop, Walk the Dog, and some with no names, on and on he twirled and finessed the spinning things, and never once broke a string. His spangled aerobatics in the spring sunshine mesmerized them, struck them dumb. On top of which he announced he wasn't selling anything.

FOR A WHILE ON BIRTHDAYS THE OTHER BOYS had a ritual of spanking the birthday clown, after singing Happy Birthday and blowing out candles, but before cake and presents. Shouting out the count in unison, all the hands together beating on his backside. "One, two, three, four, five, six—and one to grow on!" Beating as celebration? An extra swat for the future? How could spanking make you grow? It felt like something out of an olden time, an initiation boys passed through, that no one questioned, that someone once thought made them stronger.

THE PICNIC AT THE ZOO was eaten up and packed away. The sun had set, and they were trudging toward the parking lot, circling a pond filled with nattering ducks and swans, then came upon an airy white gingerbread building with singing inside going on. The stage was so bright it hurt their eyes, and the singing voices of women and men were huge, thrilling and powerful, soaring out in the dark over them. The audience was like one vast animal heaving and sighing, roaring its approval, then abruptly stilled. The little clowns couldn't understand one word of the songs, but were still amazed, it was so full of feeling, so alive and strong. Their mother whispered that this was an opera house. As they stood there peeking at the doings backstage, there came answering bellows and roars from across the pond, from the Elephant House, and from the Carnivores.

THE CLOWN FAMILY MOVED into a big old house late one fall, just before his mother came home from the hospital with a brand-new baby boy. They didn't have much furniture, and at the moment no mom, so the place felt huge and hollow. And the furnace didn't work, so when the mom and baby arrived they set up the one big bed in the living room of this chilly barn, built up a roaring fire in the fireplace big enough to roast an ox. The clown boys fed and kept it burning nonstop for days till the furnace men finally showed up to fix what was wrong. Then the dad announced he was going shopping for furniture. But the mom was afraid of his wild grand borrowing, said she couldn't sleep in a bed he hadn't paid cash for, she would never get her rest for fear the bed might be snatched out from under them. So next morning the dad went straight to the bank and borrowed more money, but cash this time, then went and bought their new bed. He told her he paid cash, and she never asked where he got it. They were both country people who'd moved to town, who'd already come far, but some things just weren't done. This was how they negotiated a big bad world that would always threaten to swallow them. The young clown studied their deal on the bed and thought he understood, years before it dawned on him.

FIRST THE MUSIC CAME ON, then an announcer with the morning news, then flashing lights for a while, then beeping. It was the fanciest alarm clock he'd ever seen, but his dad could sleep through anything. So when he and his brother were sent up to wake him, they'd start shaking his shoulder, playing a little game. Dad? Uh-huh. Can we have a bb-gun? Uh-huh. Can we have a pony? Uh-huh. Can we have a ride to the moon? Uh-huh. Choking back giggles, they knew they couldn't ask to burn down the house, but he'd give practically anything, to get to sleep one more minute.

AS THE FIRSTBORN KID in a large and active brood, he saw how his brothers and sisters needed him to mimic, agree and disagree with. They needed a sparring partner, needed their thoughts taken seriously, their jokes laughed at. They didn't need to be shushed, or given lessons in manners. Tending them as babies was easy, their needs immediate and obvious. It only got tough when they needed someone to borrow shirts and thoughts from, to wear as their own. Someone to push back against, someone with a little sense and competence, but not too much. One winter day they stole his wool cap and scarf and gloves to make a snowman, and were so delighted with the likeness he didn't get his things back till the snow melted and they'd shrunk to fit the thieves.

HIS LITTLE SISTER LOVED BABY BIRDS. She would find one fallen or heaved from the nest, fix a shoebox full of grass, get an eyedropper of milk and care for it till it perished. He even climbed a ladder for her with the half-naked thing cheeping in his shirt pocket, to put back in its nest in the gutter, wearing gloves since everybody knew if you handled a bird, the parents would smell your touch and have no more to do with it. Finally the little sister admitted that she had found some baby birds in a low nest in the bushes, and when no one was looking, not even the mommy, had touched them. Over the years science finally discovered that birds had no sense of smell. Even buzzards relied on their eyesight to spot flies on roadkill, to let them know it was ripe. But in later life the little girl clown could hardly feel the secret joy of playing with those birds—what she felt still mostly guilt.

HIS LITTLE SISTER ALSO LOVED CLOWNING, making people laugh, but didn't yet understand jokes. So he told her to go tell the grownups to ask her what she wanted to be when she grew up, and told her to answer A big red firetruck. When she did, the roar of laughter astonished and frightened her. She fell down on the floor, burst out crying, said I don't want to be a big red firetruck, he made me say that! So he promised: No more funny lessons.

THE FAMILY HAD TWO MEALTIME RULES: no singing at the dinner table, and no reading except for Sunday morning funnies. Otherwise these little birds were apt to break into song at the drop of a hat, and all might join in, or else get food in their books, and stick the pages together.

HE THOUGHT OF COUNTRY LIFE as slow and quiet, but also comforting, safe. Things went along like they'd always been for his grandparents in their little post office and general store, where farmers would come in, count their change, poke around. The wider world rarely intruded, and then word would come to them from afar, in the evenings gathered round the radio. There might be shushing to hear of the latest doings in Congress, or a stock market wobble, or weather so fierce somewhere else, an earthquake or flood or cold snap. What happened here was never so dramatic—a rare surprise like when someone staked out a pony to eat down the lush grass in the ditch outside the cemetery. Right away he wondered why they hadn't put the pony in among the tombstones, that had a good strong fence and grass aplenty. When he asked, someone said It weren't proper, letting it walk on the graves.

THERE WERE COUNTRY ROADS TO NOWHERE but other fields and woods with now and then a lone barn or house oasis, a tight knot of old trees. Little towns with four or five houses, a storefront. Towns so small at the last house the rutted gravel quit. Sometimes the town was an island or in winter might as well be, with nothing around to tempt you even as an excuse not to stay put. Where if you went out you soon had to turn back or make your own way, first on rock and sand, then over frozen water.

COUNTRY FOLKS THOSE DAYS STILL BROKE DOWN and wore out. The old ones that could get around walked with a limp. That was part of the wages of work, of going at it tooth and nail eight days a week. Yes, there was a letup in winter, when all you could do was sleep long and keep warm on the side facing the fire. Kept breaking the skin on the water trough, made sure the animals were fed enough to carry through till the new green showed itself. Meanwhile, living depended on what you had saved and stacked up, canned or fermented, frozen, smoked or dried. That you watched and doled out, figured close as you could.

ON THE CLAPBOARD WALL OUTSIDE THE KITCHEN on the glassed-in back porch was the spot where for generations all the kids were measured. Every family used to have such a spot, where endless neat staggered notations piled up. A catalog of nearly everyone but the most ancient, all their visits growing up, that said here you mattered. The ritual was performed with a book teetering atop the head, sighted square and true, beneath which the line was penciled, followed by the name and date. No kid ever had to be told Stand up straight. Some even wore their fat shoes, forgot they were always measured in their stocking feet.

AFTER GRANDMA DIED OF LEUKEMIA his grandfather got gangrene from an infected toe and had to have his leg cut off. He'd sit rocking on the porch of his store, look out across the road to the cemetery where his name and birthdate were carved in advance on a double headstone alongside the wife he sorely missed, gone now several years. As Catholics, they had buried his leg in his spot in a box with its own blessing, so come Judgment Day the risen body parts could find each other. The old man told of phantom pains in the lost leg, itches he couldn't scratch. And sometimes joked about having one foot in the grave. The clown asked why he didn't get a wooden leg but got no answer. He wondered how his grandpa could stand those rubber-tipped crutches that forced you to stagger and plant yourself.

STARING INTO THE GRAIN OF THE TABLE, rocking into the grain of the floor, such fixity none dared call despair. When the boy would edge close, ask how he was, he'd say Waiting for the Lord to take me. Then lift his head, give that look. In denial still a presence, a steady gaze, though when his grown daughters laid the open violin case in his lap he wouldn't touch it, wouldn't flick a string to see was it anywhere near in tune. Even kept waiting in the dark an age, no chance it might be coaxed back to life.

HE SNUCK IN TO SEE if his old one-legged grandfather was taking a nap like he was supposed to. But he was lying there in the darkened room watching shadows cross the ceiling, feeling the shade flutter in the open window, listening to whatever else was stirring around the house and store. The boy said Aren't you tired? The old man said Yes, but I don't like to sleep much. When the boy said Why not, he said Afraid I might miss something.

HE SAT DOWN BY THE OLD MAN ROCKING one day, asked what he did for fun as a boy. His grandfather looked at him and shook his head, then told about going to a state teachers' convention, nearly a day's drive upstate, what with roads like they were in those days. He'd already been teaching for years, said he was smack in the middle of his life, but this was the first thing of the kind he had done. He spent the night before and the night after in a college dormitory, and on the way home the next day stopped for a snack and some gas. Another man pulled in behind him and while they waited for the attendant they got to talking. Turned out the other man was a teacher too, had been to the same convention. They swapped stories about what they'd seen and heard and done. When they parted they shook hands and introduced themselves. He found this teacher about the same age, who had lived and taught his whole life just forty miles away, shared the same first and last name.

HIS FAVORITE MAIDEN AUNT was all the other cousins' favorite too. She was generous, gave them more time than their parents could, listened to their laments and despairs, their secret dreams and joys. She seemed to have an eye on everything they did. The cousins were careful of her feelings, wouldn't play Old Maid around her, though she was likely where they'd learned the game in the first place. He never understood why she had no husband or kids of her own, why she took care of her aging parents till they died. But she was needed, and that was what she did. She brought the first modern appliance into her parents' home, a little four-burner propane gas stove tucked in a corner where it wouldn't seem to compete with her mother's green enamel wood cookstove that could feed an army and usually did. She worked at a whiskey distillery, sang solos in the church choir, owned a nice new car, took vacations to far-away places, and had one secret no one else knew but the clown. Though she wore glasses, she had an eye for four-leaf clovers, as she put it, and on picnics would find them with an ease that embarrassed her. She told him it wasn't luck, there was no trick to it, she just looked and there they were.

WOMEN SOUNDED DIFFERENT BACK THEN. The clown knew country women whose voices seemed strangled, half-swallowed as if all they said were wrenched out of silence, a sob. There were town women whose voices were brassy, whose laughter was raucous, throaty and raw as crow talk. There were whiskey tenors sanded down by drink and menthol cigarettes. And there were liquid little-girl murmurs burbling like water over stones, reedy flutes out of thickets and sighing half-whispers he could scarcely follow, all manner of self-denial and baby-talk before women were listened to, persistently asked what they wanted, what they thought.

THE DAY CAME WHEN HE GOT GOOD ENOUGH on his bike that he asked his mom what she needed from the store. She smiled, said we could use another loaf of sandwich bread, gave him some money, and off he pedaled. The store was further off than church and school, but he knew the way, and flew like the wind. He bought the right bread with the square thinner slices, but didn't get an extra bag since the bread came in its own plastic bag. He set off for home, but didn't get far before trouble caught up with him. First he held the bread against the handlebars with his grip on the mouth of the bag, but wobbling and bouncing along the bread soon settled into a ball. So he stopped to fluff it up and rearrange it, then tried holding it lightly by the square middle, but that soon squished it till the loaf got to be like a dumbbell. He stopped again, tried as best he could to shape it right, then tucked it inside his T-shirt so he could steer with both hands. But pedaling along his shirttail pulled loose and the bread slipped out and hit the road. When he tried to unsquish it now it was worse than ever, a couple of flattened pear shapes with a skinny neck in the middle. He even laid it out on a car hood to try and fix the pieces. By now half the loaf was scraps and crumbs. The rest of the ride home was spent figuring what else he could have done. If he had more money he'd have bought another loaf, got cardboard and string and tied it to the handlebars, fed this one to the birds and said nothing. The hardest part was not crying when he handed her the shapeless hopeless thing that she should have laughed at but didn't, read in an instant what happened.

WHEN HE STARTED GOING OVER to friends' houses, the clown's good manners drew compliments but he wasn't fooled. It just meant he looked grownups in the eye and talked to them, asked questions and waited for answers, because he mostly found them full of clues about how things really worked, that they wouldn't tell you at school. Grown-ups were playing in the big game while he was benchwarming, swimming in the deep end while he was stuck in the wading pool. He knew most people wanted to talk about themselves, found you interesting to the extent that you showed an interest. So you nodded in agreement, coaxed them to say more than they meant to, spill the beans.

A MONTH INTO SCHOOL HE WAS ASSIGNED a new friend who spoke no English. The teacher plunked him down alongside and said Do what you can. With pale skin, black hair and eyes, Josef was tall and skinny as he was, intense and curious. By the end of the first day he had a dozen or twenty new words. Out on the front steps the clown quizzed him, pointing out street and car, tree and window and door. After two weeks with broken sentences Josef invited the clown home with him, to the oldest, poorest part of town. To a four-story tenement that surrounded a courtyard with weeds growing up through the bricks, with garden patches that still held a few cabbages and potatoes and dead flowers, with broken furniture stacked against walls under tarps. There he had tea with sugar cubes with the family in their gloomy front room without lights. Their windows on the third floor faced a brick wall several feet off. He learned that in a family of three generations, six people, Josef had the only English, that he was sharing as fast as he could. While the grownups buzzed softly around their ears, he gathered they were from Yugoslavia, refugees who had had to leave, stealing out in the night with what they could carry and wear. While the boys traded postage stamps he learned that their homeland had several different names, that for fifty years had kept changing. While the boys held up stamps to the candlelight, his mama cooked a pot of something with paprika, vinegar and rice, that was pungent and tasty. Josef gave him some of his favorite old stamps, that had King Alexander's portrait rimmed in black for mourning, used for years after his death. He had made it clear to Josef that he wanted to learn his language too, but the boy was so feverish to talk English, they never got beyond the first few words of greeting and goodbye.

THE YOUNG CLOWN WAS TREATED to liberal doses of Humility, a non-specific cure spooned into him like cod-liver oil, meant to counter brightness and speed on the uptake, ready retention of the odd fact, puzzle, daydream, conjecture. It was a time-honored Catholic remedy thought to be good for what ailed the tender springtime soul, as well as a parenting medicine. But it could be overdone, when used to treat nearly everything. The young patient could be too cleansed and purged and beaten down, rendered too obedient to recall whose life this was, that fun had a purpose, jokes flavored lessons hard to swallow otherwise.

HIS FIRST OVERNIGHT CAMPING TRIP was the Polar Bear, with snow on the ground, with mittens, earflaps, long underwear. He was ten and a half, a Webelos who didn't have a sleeping bag, but they showed him how to make a bed roll of two blankets folded and fixed with diaper pins, bundled in an old shower curtain. Most kids used Army surplus pup tents, proud of doing it like their dads and uncles in WWII and Korea, where each soldier was issued a shelter half to button together with a buddy's to make a whole tent. With half a tent and one pole you had to find a buddy or were out of luck. Most of that first night below freezing he was up shivering, drinking cocoa around a gas lantern that sat huffing and glaring, that needed pumping up every little while. There was a whiskey smell to the grownups, a lot of flapping and stamping, talk about sticking your tongue on a frosty pump handle, and spitting at forty below, how it crackled and froze in midair.

AFTER A TOUR OF THE FIREHOUSE with his firefighter scoutmaster, the young clown laid out his clothes like a fireman, to jump in all set for the day. Pants and shirt and socks and shoes just so, that he practiced throwing on and off to get the time down. He even craved a shiny brass pole to slide, since running stairs could cost a tumble, but the folks just laughed and said Slow down.

THEIR SCOUTMASTER LIKED TO PLAY Ghosties in the twilight. They'd pick out a tree for home base, count to a hundred while he disappeared, then go looking for him. Lurking in the bushes with a bag of flour in his pocket, when he caught someone sneaking close he'd hit the kid with a handful, turn him into a ghosty who was out of the game. Finally there would be just the old jungle-soldier-firefighter in the shadows running for the tree, having used up the last of his ammo, with a few kids still scrambling to tag him.

THE DOZEN LONG-STEMMED WHITE ROSES arrived swathed in green tissue paper in a long green box delivered by a guy in a matching green truck and uniform, which the clown never opened, just put it in the freezer by the back door and forgot. Later when asked if anything had come that special day, their anniversary two weeks after Pearl Harbor, three days before Christmas, he still forgot. Until his father described the box—then he ran to get the roses, which by then were blackened and silvered.

HE AND HIS BROTHER AND SISTER WENT FISHING with Dad, a rare outing halfway across the state in the middle of the night to a huge lake rumored to have muskies, though none of them had ever seen one that wasn't mounted and stuffed. He had climbed in the back seat to catch a little shut-eye when a weaving padiddle came at them down the two-lane highway. His dad pulled off the right shoulder but the car kept sliding over, crushed in the left side of their car, bounced off and kept going. The cops arrived as he was picking glass out of his head. They had caught a one-eyed drunk driver down the road with the left side of his car bashed in, all covered with cream-colored paint. Their car still ran, though they had to climb in the right side, and with the sun coming up, they decided to go fishing anyhow, since they still had a can of nightcrawlers, a bag of baloney sandwiches, and had come all this way. They rented a kicker boat and caught a bucket of mud cats, bluegills and croppies and sunburns and not much else. When they got home late in the day after all that driving, his dad stopped at the street, made the kids get out of the car, walk up and ring the doorbell, while he backed the car up the curvy driveway so mom couldn't see the wrecked side of the car until she knew they were safe.

HE WAS 12, READING THE SUNDAY PAPER, a front-page article about the latest crime statistics. Burglary, armed robbery, aggravated assault. He looked up and asked his mother what was rape. She said You'll have to ask your father—who was still upstairs asleep. He promptly forgot and moved on to the funnies. A couple hours later when his father came down, he said he wanted to talk, led him into his study and closed the door. There the ceiling fell in on him, all this heavy technical talk of vaginas and penises, eggs and sperms and fetuses, the mechanics of making babies. It took half an hour to even think what this might be about. His father never did explain rape, just got to the outskirts of love, stuff about how you might meet a person that felt special, how both of you might want to show how you felt, hold hands and kiss, but any more would have to wait for marriage. For years he had no clue and didn't want to know what "any more" even meant.

IT WAS TIME TO BUY SHOES AGAIN, but the young clown didn't want clodhoppers any more. No one but he and his brother wore those black high-top work shoes, that spoke of roaming farms and climbing barns, of work in the hot sun and rough-and-tumble play. He liked their common-sense ruggedness, though their schoolmates mocked and laughed. This time amid pleadings and tears once more their parents insisted, and next day walking home from school in the new shoes he got caught in a gullywasher that soaked him to the skin, made every step go squishy, stained his feet blue for a week. The shoes made a mournful melody, sounded like a pair of ducks lost in fog, calling plaintively back and forth, Where are we, where are we, left right left. That soon had him stomping through puddles, gurgling and nattering back.

SUMMER BEFORE EIGHTH GRADE AT 13 all at once he grew up. Got big as he was going to get. Skinny as a rail but six foot one, biggest kid in the school. His work boots from then on got resoled and heeled for the next twenty years, till they rotted apart, got filled with dirt, planted in hens and chicks, given away as a present. In school for the first time boys wanted to fight and jumped him out of the blue to prove he wasn't so tough. Roughhousing was one thing, but if it wasn't fair, something in him took over, wouldn't let him get the worst of it.

FOR A WHILE HE FELT like Boppo the Clown. Always getting hit, but bouncing right back up with a little Ha-ha that didn't hurt none. That made them want to nail him harder next time. Sure he saw stars, but loved the bounce built into him. Till eventually it felt like they knocked the air out, popped something, taught him to play rug, stay down till they were gone. Which was no lesson, might as well have been printed on the box he came in, a caution against excessive force, that might take the fun out of everything.

48

HE GREW SO FAST HIS BRAINS BUBBLED UP through his haircut like cookie dough, like a box of bisquick baked by boy scouts in an army helmet. His feet yawned and stretched, his shirtsleeves hiked to his elbows, his pants cuffs crawled to his knees, his legs ran away with him, his arms windmilled the sky. The grinning snouts of his shoes showed his curious toes. Lucky he didn't get much bigger around. Suddenly almost everyone was looking up to him, or pretending to study his belt buckle, the one worn thing that still fit. The old folks talked of growing pains, of hot summer nights hearing corn stretch and crackle, and somewhere in there he read Rip Van Winkle, who slept for twenty years because he went night-bowling and drank too much. And though his mother told him to stand up straight, she also stooped around short people. He had to practice looking down from this sudden dizzy height.

MOM'S COUNTRY SENSE OF HUMOR took some getting used to. Dry as the harvest you prayed for, dry as a lick of Indiana lightning without a cloud in the sky. So dry you were never sure what was even a joke, When she caught the shivers and anyone noticed, she'd say a goose just walked on my grave. And when suddenly he got big at 13, grew a foot and needed all these new clothes, he asked her if she thought he had big feet. Which, face it, were monsters. She studied him and his feet with a straight face, up and down, and said she thought he had a fine understanding. Then they both laughed.

HE GOT DEATHLY ILL FOR A STRETCH. His parents were worried enough they hauled his mattress into their room, where they could keep an eye. As soon as the fever broke he asked for something to read, lay there and ran through everything they brought. Mostly piles of novels, Zane Grey, Jack London, Conan Doyle. The Autobiography of Benvenuto Cellini. And one by Bishop Fulton J. Sheen, full of gentle jokes about being good in a wicked old world. He read so much in a few days he got pinkeye, though they had a fancy name for it. Dosed him with a tube of ointment that glued his eyelashes together, that took forever to melt. There was no reading through the goop, and even TV was smeary, like looking up from the bed of a frozen lake. So he got to use his convict skills, go visit a head full of what he could recall and picture clearly, fall back on what couldn't be taken away no matter what. Too bad there were no crimes to solve.

THE EIGHTH-GRADE CLOWN HAD BEEN SICK for weeks.
While he was gone they had put him in a school pageant, gave him
lines to learn, a little speech about Lincoln. With the fever down but
still weak as a kitten he learned his speech, and when the day came he
showed up in his gray wool suit and tie. When they called his name he
went up to the podium, looked out at the four or five hundred people
on squeaky folding chairs, and froze. When he opened his mouth all the
air went out of him. There was a wheezy sigh like an accordion being
squashed. In this silly silent concert he fluttered, a moth at a porchlight.
They had to come get him, pry his fingers off the lectern, lead him stiff
and slippery away.

STILL HE GOT TO STUDY the big man's stovepipe hat and shapeless
gloves that summer in the Smithsonian. And casts of his large muscled
hands. There were glass-plate photos and scribbled famous words and
lots of other stuff, but what he wanted wasn't there, lived only in story.
He thought of sums figured on a shovel with charcoal by firelight.
Of the snowy winters at Pigeon Creek, elm-bark tied on his feet for
shoes. Of the mother abruptly taken by milk fever, buried there. Of the
summer-long trip of two boys to New Orleans on a flatboat, that showed
him slaves and masters, let him practically taste the whip and chains.
The fabled wrestling moves of that lanky boy, that made him unbeat-
able. And woven through stories he told, his abrupt and raucous laugh.

THAT SUMMER BEFORE HIGH SCHOOL he read Uncle Tom's
Cabin. That he knew even then was propaganda, meant to make him
feel certain ways, rather than giving him facts, letting him make up his
mind. A favorite scene that always strained credulity and reminded him
it was written, not lived, was Eliza crossing the Ohio River on ice floes,
on the run north from slavers and their dogs. With her little boy in her
arms, she leapt from floe to floe, and never jumped till there was another
to land on, that always arrived just in time.

STILL, AT 13 HE DIDN'T ALWAYS THINK things through. He
was straightening a horseshoe on a boulder with a sledgehammer, that
bounced up and caught him between the eyes. He woke with two
lumps on his head, front and back, studying the blue sky through sway-

ing maple leaves. It took a minute to remember where he was, what he'd nearly done. That lucky horseshoe stayed crooked.

AFTER DARK THEY HID IN THE BUSHES and rolled out a dented chrome hubcap just as a car hit the intersection that came at a little dip. It was a dirty trick that seemed harmless at the moment. The car would slam on its brakes, the driver would hop out, look at his wheel covers, find none missing, turn to the bushes and shake his fist. But this time the guy heard the hubcap clatter and hit his brakes at a green light and just missed the guy running a red light into him, a miss close enough to peel paint. Just sat there shaking and staring. And the clowns playing god never laughed.

THERE WAS AN ANCIENT CLOWN in his neighborhood, formal in suit, vest, homburg and spats, stout cane he counted on, skinny, unsteady and frail. In fall the man would pick his way slowly along a straight level sidewalk, and work himself into a towering rage attacking acorns and pinecones and fallen leaves in his path. It was a battle waged with demons in miniature, a tempest in a teapot that could have been a circus act spun in a spotlight to a hot calliope. One afternoon walking home the boy found himself directly behind the old man, realized he was hard of hearing, tried not to follow too close, but still overheard what the old man spewed forth. Not that he knew what it meant. It wasn't English or French, not Spanish, German, Italian. With no real target in sight, the old clown tightly stoppered, sealed in a rage that might pop his lid to get free, the boy fell back and crossed the street, to pass unnoticed by.

FOR A WHILE HE DIDN'T THINK ANY PICTURE taken of him looked like him, like how he saw himself. And his bad sides all overlapped. There was that end-on shot of him eating a candy cane, that made his mouth a perfect white O of astonishment. He got to think of picture-taking as a conspiracy to embarrass people, a game to catch each other looking silly. When someone gave him a camera, he pretended to like it, but then hid the one-eyed thing in his underwear drawer. The Indians were right—cameras could steal your soul, turn you into this stiff wooden thing that couldn't fly or sing, got mocked even selling cigars. Then he surrendered to the obvious, saw how each picture showed what it caught, told its limited truth. Even blurry, fired off at the clouds or your toes. While time waltzed away uninvited, like a bear at a picnic.

WATCHING THE LAST STEAM ENGINE pull out of town in 1955, no telling how he should feel. Was this what nostalgia meant, chuffing plumes of smoke, billows of steam near the ground, showers of cinders and sparks, drive wheels hammering as they spun then gathered traction and bit, eased away slowly trailing a melancholy wail? It was a flawed way to go, rained grit and fire in its passing, but even so here was met with solemn waves down the line, from engineer and fireman up front to conductor on the platform at the end. The beast a gleaming manicured beauty, huffing like a distance runner on his last legs, seductive but hopeless.

ONE FALL AFTERNOON THEY SNUCK into a hobo camp in the woods past the north end of the rail yard. The boys tried to be invisible. The hobos were mostly bearded, dirty and ragged, already wearing all their clothes in layers. It seemed like each one had his own little nest in the bushes, made of cardboard and tin, plywood and plastic. They lounged around a fire where several tramps were cooking up something in a blackened old lard can. One was pulling the skin off a rabbit with pliers, another was cutting up carrots and onions and potatoes with a rusty machete he sharpened on a brick. One was opening tin cans with an ax, shucking corn likely swiped out of somebody's garden. Most were drinking, some already far gone, so the recipe was improvised. Whatever they had they threw in, and after a while it started to smell pretty good. There were no women around. Never mind jobs and banks, this was how men might live if there were no soap or toilets, no sisters or moms. One started to sing, but the words got away from him.

THEY KNEW BLACKY, who looked like a hobo but wasn't one any-more. He had settled down after a fashion, was a track checker, got a little money for walking a few miles of rails with his eyes and ears open twice a week, reporting what needed fixing. In the woods he'd built himself a little squatter's shack of rusty tin signs just his height, twice the size of his mattress, with a little stove and a couple shelves, with everything he owned by way of clothes and tools hanging on one or another of a dozen nails. In dry weather he cooked outside in a saucepan or skillet, squatting over the coals. He got his water from a spring up the hillside, that no one else knew about. All his tools had handles he'd made himself. He said he knew which woods to use, and once he made one it never wore out or broke.

ONE DAY HE ASKED BLACKY where he came from, where was home. The little man went into his shack, came out with a photo of a plump young woman in a bonnet holding a little boy's hand, standing in front of a white clapboard house with a picket fence. He said They died in the fire, that took everything. I been on the road ever since.

COUNTRY KIDS USED TO RUN AWAY and join the circus, back when they still performed in tents and rode on trains. These kids knew all about chores, feeding and herding animals, lifting heavy weights, and their shy innocence made them prime clown material. What could be better than making oneself useful, living on the road in disguise, while he figured who or what he was? Perfecting clown tricks like cracking a peanut with a sledge-hammer or balancing an ostrich feather on his nose, could mount up over time to an act they might want in the show.

THEN ALL AT ONCE THERE WAS SPUTNIK, and the Russians crowed, triumphant. It passed over every 93 minutes for three months before it sagged down into the atmosphere and burned up. That fall into winter American kids and grownups looked for it in the night sky, baffled, speech-less. They watched and listened for the beeping shiny ball moving steady on its course, beaming with reflected light, out ahead of the looming second-stage rocket that had heaved it into orbit. The ball couldn't do much but say Here I Am so ham operators could track it, but that was plenty for starters, showed them how small their Spaceship Earth truly was.

STILL IN UNLIKELY SPOTS HE FOUND CLUES how to live, would pounce on a windfall unbruised and savor it. Somewhere he read how Parisians on their days off would dress up in coat and tie to go fishing on the Seine, pack bread and cheese and wine and a folding chair, and some days couldn't be bothered baiting a hook. But what did that mean? Fishing as a kind of excuse, a sign that read Do Not Dis-turb Me With Failure and Success? That one could choose to sit and feel one's heartbeat, draw a slow deep breath, savor clouds on the water, study the flow till one could hold himself suspended against its ceaseless compulsions like a fish? One day he concluded it might be essential to seem clownish, irrelevant, oblivious, in order to crack mysteries tough as walnuts half-hidden in the grass.

growing up

"I think I'll be a clown when I get grown," said Dill. "Yes, sir, a clown....There ain't one thing in this world I can do about folks except laugh, so I'm gonna join the circus and laugh my head off." "You got it backwards, Dill," said Jem. "Clowns are sad, it's folks that laugh at them." "Well, I'm gonna be a new kind of clown. I'm gonna stand in the middle of the ring and laugh at the folks." --Harper Lee, To Kill a Mockingbird

HE KNEW HE WAS GROWING UP when he started to like fishing without live bait, when he could fool fish with a wiggly swimming lure rather than a bite of dinner hiding a hook. It was harder still to use a twitchy surface lure that floated there, struggling, indecisive, making the faintest feeble ripples till an old bass couldn't stand it and struck. Toughest of all were trout in a fast clear stream, miles from any road. Wild enough you had to sneak up, couldn't let your shadow touch the water, couldn't make a noise or they'd be spooked for hours. Then all at once he was a meat fisherman with a watch strapped on, all business and no sport.

HIS FIRST DENTIST HAD SEVERAL FLAWS. The man was kind-hearted, backed off when he caused pain, and didn't dig deep for decay. So by his mid-twenties the clown would have to have all his fillings redone. This dentist sucked breath mints, and had Muzak piped into his office, so would hum and suck while he worked, though he was tone-deaf. The clown tried to make the man to stop humming and sucking by means of questions that worked like depth charges, timed to sink to the floor of the mind and explode. One day he told the dentist he'd read about milk cows in New Jersey fitted with stainless steel teeth, because the sandy soil wore their teeth out while they still had a good dozen years. Then he asked how much to pull all his teeth and give him a stainless steel smile. Think of the shine! That day the man didn't hum or suck at all.

THE BIRTHDAY SPICE WAS THAT HINT of candle wax over icing. A spatter from the huffing that the family couldn't help but get a taste of. The greater the delay in wish-making, admiring the blaze while pondering what to wish for, the stronger the flavor of those tiny melted candles. He never thought of a wish in advance, found the wishing moment discombobulating, so pretended to think of a secret heart's desire, because he felt he didn't want or need one, should let someone else have his wish, for all the good it might do them. And looking round the table he'd pick a sad-eyed recipient, the donation secret as the wish itself.

THE SURGICAL SCRATCH and squeaky-clean break of cut glass were music to his ears. His high-school physics teacher had said glass was a liquid that took centuries to flow. He just got to fix the first window he broke, dug out the hard old putty, measured and cut the new glass. At the table's edge made a perfect snap. Then he set in the new pane, pushed down the clips, rolled a long putty snake and smooshed it in all around. But just as he was finishing, someone outside called his name, and he turned and put his elbow through the new one. Though it took half the time to do over, he polished it gently, and gave it plenty of room.

HE GOT A JOB WITH AN OLD FARMER who, when he talked at all, talked slow. Maybe tongue-tied, out of practice, maybe tasting an ancient rusty residue on the long-held tongue. So he learned to wait the old man out, not rush in shaking the handful of ants aswarm in his mental jar. When he asked something, he tried to offer several spare little questions at once, like twigs to feed a fire, then shut up, let him crackle and flash in the silence, no matter how long it took. So while they forked manure or stacked bales with all the time in the world, the young clown practiced listening, while the old farmer remembered how much fun it was to trade flapjacks like this. Pour a sizzle, loosen and flip.

FOR THE FIRST TIME SINCE SECOND GRADE he lost that clown feeling, the feeling he was beside himself, better pull himself together, quit fooling around. He was in the field on the farm building fence. Digging holes by hand in a rocky field with a two-handled digger, then swinging a sledge to set posts. Nothing went easy—everything about it was hard. Ground, posts, wire and steeples and come-along.

And you couldn't just make half a fence, any more than you could fence half a cow. And he was tired before they got started. Half a fence looked like plenty for one day. But as the day crept on and the shadows reached for him he crept too, head-down leaning in, till by dark they had wire up and down the whole line, four shiny strands set to sing.

FROM THE FIRST, GOING HOME to the country meant going back in time. It wasn't just that folks there were more old than young, or that things seemed to move more deliberately. Everything done had weight, every chore could be done right or wrong, but was one of a thousand small steps, not an end. Everything done seemed connected to everything else—every tree pruned or cut down and hauled took muscle, meant a plan. Where to split and stack, how long to dry till it would burn. Cutting grass left grass to be raked or composted, or dried, baled and fed. Every doing had consequences, that's just how it was.

THE FARM MADE SUMMER FEEL long in the right ways, down endless corn rows and days. Not a drag waiting wishing things would change but a time full of doing and growing, days that opened out not in, that made him surprise himself and those who thought they knew him. There was the look on their faces the first time he went for the tractor, walked half a mile to get it and chugged back, hooked a log chain to pull the car out of that muddy ditch. He'd known the day would come when he'd be set apart, and all at once here he was—rail-thin at fifteen, muddy-booted, serious.

DOING CHORES HE LEARNED how firewood mattered, who felled and bucked it, how it got hauled, split and stacked. A rare thing you could still say grew on trees yet wasn't free. Even if you owned the trees the getting cost sweat and chainsaw juice. Everyone who swung an ax knew to say it warmed you twice. Also knew how much of its energy went straight up the chimney, to warm and smoke up the countryside, while at every window and door the stove sucked cold air, that swirled like field mice around the warm room.

THE DIRT WAS DIFFERENT EACH DAY, as the farm stirred awake round its one precondition, its living premise, its gift. Some of it was always open, or about to be. Some mornings some was flaky, some still shined by yesterday's plow, or crumbled by the cultivator, or was mud in the rain left untouched. It was only there to be worked if dry enough. Otherwise you did chores and repairs, marked time till the fields firmed up enough to get back to. And after planting seed you held your breath till, harmless, drowsy and brave, up poked the first hint of green.

EVENTUALLY THE OLD FARMER would end up spilling the beans about everything. It was easier working alongside, pitching hay and manure, not looking the other in the eye. There was only one unspoken rule, you paid in coin of the realm. Story for story, truth for truth. No questions without answering yourself. Sometimes the flat slap of truth seemed to hurt, but not long, the trades mostly kid stuff. Out of a time fifty years before he was born, he heard of a world without motorcars, aeroplanes or World Wars, how boys buckled their knickers, games they played, Knockers with a buckeye on a string, outhouse jokes they told, heroes and villains in the time of McKinley and Roughrider Teddy Roosevelt. Bill was just his age, 15, when he saw his first car, a Willys Overland, and 20 before he rode in a Ford Model T touring car.

THE TWO OLD FARMERS WERE HAVING fun with him, but it was also work running their mouths nonstop while he shoveled three tons of sand off the truck. If they'd stopped talking they might have had to take a turn for old time's sake. So they wondered was it harder to dig dry sand or wet sand, as they pointed out samples of each. Wet sand was neater, every bite stuck together so you could take a bigger bite, which the water made heavier, so that you shoveled more weight. Dry sand was light but loose. In any wind it would drift and blow all over. He went back and forth with the shovel, trying this and that since it all had to go anyhow, determined not to laugh when they said he should keep the dry on top like cake icing, and dig the wet chocolate cake out from under.

SHE PAUSED ON THE TRACKS to look both ways, and stalled the car. In the country the woods were leafed out, there was no seeing round the curve. His mother had waited till her 40s to learn to drive, even after he did, and for her the whole thing was edgy, frightening. He saw she'd flooded it, told her to hold the pedal down to the floor and crank it over. He could hear the train coming somewhere behind that green veil, was getting set to snatch the little ones out of the back when it roared to life and she threw it into gear.

HIS PARENTS WERE BOTH COUNTRY PEOPLE determined to leave behind the dirt, sweat and worry. But that past came in handy, and some old ways lingered. His dad knew fruits and vegetables and cuts of meat, knew to sniff the scar of the stem on a melon, knew to kill and pluck a chicken so quick his hands blurred in motion. And his mother with a few offhand questions could get the story out of anyone, sort through polite chitchat and see what was what as if she were still rocking on her parents' porch, snapping beans for supper, shelling peas.

THEN THE CLOWN'S MOM WAS FINISHED. A bad stomach that mostly had to be cut out, an eighth pregnancy discovered while preparing for surgery, a premature baby girl, then a ride to the end through a summer and fall of distractions, gentle games, pretenses that fooled no one but the very young. Plain and simple living out of the common pot, about like a hobo camp. Not many jokes—the drugs those days never good enough. Her suffering and decline though obvious went unremarked, hardly hidden even from the little ones. Who knows what the sensible thing to do would have been. The clown babysat, played with the little ones, fed them and told stories, and in-between carved a menagerie out of bars of Ivory soap. With the bars he'd bought all the same size, there was no way of keeping any sense of scale. The dozen animals lined the kitchen window near where she lay—elephant, rhino, hippo, giraffe, rabbit and mouse, on and on—till one day his little brother decided to play with them, found them stuck to the wood, and one by one pulled all the bodies off the legs. So they hobbled to the soap dish upstairs, and dissolved in bathtub games.

THE ONE PERSONAL MOMENT THEY HAD was an apology. Out of the blue she took him aside when he came in from school, said she knew she had been short with him over the winter—her words—and that she was sorry. He didn't yet know her operation was only days away. They had just learned what was wrong, what would have to be cut out to give her any chance. He said there was nothing to apologize for, recalled a few sudden upwellings of anger fired off at the world, that he had precious little to do with. He didn't ask what was really going on, just kept his head down, his hands busy.

SHE COULDN'T SAY GOODBYE. Maybe because eight were too many, the weight too great. Maybe she was caught, too schooled to be kind, her fine instincts too muddied by fear and pain. In the hospital room she did talk with her eldest daughter, who turned eleven that summer, saw needs in the girl she could meet—and though it might be too early, there was only now. But while you could draw breath, how form the word goodbye? How hold still for feelings you'd mostly been able to laugh off, or play poker with? How face all that work left undone, all those bright little bundles of instinct set in a row, their hair neatly brushed, their clothes on straight for the moment? So they dressed up and stood one last time outside her hospital window—all waved, while unseen she studied them through the screen.

THEN CAME HER FUNERAL, that proved itself all for the living, let the dead bury their dead. Nobody thought that so many would come. But here they all were in their 40s come to look in the mirror in the open box, like her hitting their stride just as they were starting to feel tired, their real work yet to be done. The church offered her as pale exemplar, the consolation of heaven. But there was not a public word about who she'd been. The clown went home afterward, sat a while with the drinkers, heard the sweet things said of her in private, then went up to bed and wrote about his father, his first serious poem about that strength he'd need in days to come. None of them seemed to know how much of that strength had been her quietly standing among them, making of herself a shelter, holding up off them the weight of the world. Now no stopping the heavy tent coming down.

MOURNING WAS ONE THING nobody talked about, not old people, not kids. No answering how you lived with a hole in you that never closed. How you held yourself up like a tree split by storms, that tried to grow its ragged edges together over loss, heal a purposeless emptiness. How were you to quit missing the one who had held the answers, set the agenda and mood for the day's work and play? The family began taking turns stepping into the limelight, playing good girl or bad boy, asking to be knocked down or lifted. But it was nothing like the real thing, pebbles in a bucket rattling round an empty game.

HE NEVER BOTHERED ASKING ANYONE why did she have to die. The simple fact was enough to cancel reason and doubt, and extinguish prayer. Everything she was and did were what her eight young ones had to lose, though they didn't know that yet, would only learn in years to come, when for one then another, human connections drifted off or fell apart. Nothing thickened or annealed the slender strand of living. There was a chance to carry on, but nothing came easy, or once fled ever doubled back. Plain living countenanced the shallowing of one's breath, the clutch of fear, the freeze to escape detection, the wait on disaster by the highway like an all-night convenience store. He felt like a cabbie pulled over in an empty part of town with his meter running, half-hoping to be paid, but with the car in gear, his foot poised to hit the gas.

AFTER HIS MOTHER WAS GONE most afternoons after school he would play with the little ones gently and long. The youngest weren't in school yet, so would have been waiting forever. Their favorite game was Dogpile, a roll on the rug where they'd kick off their shoes and he'd lie down and let them pile on, climb all over him. No kicking, no tickling, a noisy tumbling embrace in slow motion that giggled and popped like a campfire, gave and took what they'd missed, couldn't get enough of any more.

DRIVING BACK FROM THE COUNTRY one Sunday night their dad had been drinking, and at a little bridge without guard rails he fishtailed on gravel and hung the right rear wheel out over the crick. The teen clown and his brother got out of the car full of little ones, without a word tried lifting and rocking the car back onto the road, but it was too heavy. So they stacked wet rocks up against the wheel, and found a fence post to pry against the frame, lift and lean into. While they sweated and strained their dad spun the wheels and sprayed them with gravel, till the rear wheel climbed back up onto the road. They got back in and on he drove, all the way home slow and silent, sensing a near miss that had made the two clowns feel expendable.

HE STOPPED TO WATCH SPARROWS take a dust bath in a sunny patch on the trail. Fluffing feathers, squabbling endlessly. Spreading their wings to the dust, then shaking them out, doubling in size for a moment, then grooming, settling back down into themselves. He knew what they were up to, suffocating mites, but beyond that who were they?

They sounded like a country family on washday making a game out of laundry, or like kids at a swimming hole, eight or nine noisy little birds, all but identical. Oblivious to his presence, till he took one more step. Then at once in one motion, one flash of wings they were gone.

ONE SUNDAY MORNING HE CAME ACROSS an article about football players doing ballet exercises. One exercise that caught his eye was one-legged deep knee bends, done between a pair of chairs to keep his balance. So he went off and tried it for himself. He did twenty or thirty on each leg, and thought he must be in pretty good shape. But next morning he could hardly get out of bed, couldn't bend his knees to pull on his pants. His thighs were burning, his muscles all knotted up. At school he couldn't walk up or down stairs, had to take them one at a time, with a pause in-between. When he got home he looked at the article again, to see if there was a catch. But it was written to tease tough guys, just said Warm up and cool down, and always point your toes.

HE FELL ASLEEP ON THE TRAIN faced forward, watching where he was going as he talked through the night with a classmate alongside. Coming back from national speech and debate finals in Baltimore, where he hadn't done great but not so bad really. After awards the participants had been given a boat ride on the Chesapeake. He'd met a Louisiana girl who was a study in enchantment, with her playful drawl and yellow summer dress with spaghetti straps and wide rustling skirts, shivering at the rail in the sunset, where he'd slipped her into his jacket. Now he was jolted awake by the train going backwards, running wide open through woods and hills. Were they driving with mirrors, or flying blind, or had they hitched an engine to the other end? He asked the conductor, learned a tunnel had caved in, so they had to backtrack eighty miles to detour through the mountains. He said the whole section was closed to let them back up all the way.

THEN EVERYWHERE HE LOOKED there were girls. He already knew mostly they got to choose, and except for tackle football that's how the game was played. But that didn't keep the choices made from feeling any less painful or ludicrous. Some girls did have dates who needed lessons in hair combing, mouth wiping, buttoning their clothes. But even neatened and cleaned up sometimes they let him know without saying, how they were just marking time till the real thing came along, like their choice was going out with him to be seen or sitting home.

THE YOUNG CLOWN WAS SLOW to figure things out, when it came to matters of love. Part of his trouble was being kept in the dark about what girls wanted and needed, what was at stake, what the game really was. Besides which, the simple mechanics of attraction and repulsion were often at odds with the most basic premise, which was how to like the ones who liked you back. He could maybe figure how to catch a short girl going up the stairs, to kiss her on the level. He could admire and praise what he liked about her hair, that might be just a cowlick to others. He could start to pay attention to what girls really laughed at, and what made them stop and go breathless. But they were still way ahead, up where the looks seemed inscrutable, complications knotted and snarled.

ONE DAY VISITING, HIS KENTUCKY GRANDMOTHER told his fortune with an ordinary deck of cards. She had him shuffle and cut the deck, then dealt out on the table the four queens face-up. Red, black, red, black. He was seventeen, had only had a couple dates, and wondered what this meant. She let out an open-mouthed cackle, said For the rest of your days you are in for woman trouble.

HE WISHED HE COULD HAVE ASKED his mom what to do about this feminine onrush—their coy looks and dazzling smiles, their moves so deft and dismissive, their sweet-smelling cleanliness, all their expense and distraction—but that chance was gone. With each of them was he only trying to replace her, find that attention, how it leaned into him like an invisible wind, a force that filled his sails, lifted and carried him? Did he suspect every one of them would tire and leave him? Was this but more of the secret mourning, the loss fated never to end?

MEANWHILE HE WAS ACTING LIKE he would live forever. Sped around cutting corners, going nights without rest. His life felt like a race to a closing door, that would slam and lock of its own weight. It felt overwhelmingly serious, this life his one chance to break free—and do what? With death already near enough to touch, he didn't yet know what that was, suspected it meant no more than what old farmers called a dirt nap. Figured why bother till it hit. But then maybe he didn't yet care enough for his life, had no notion how to belong or abide, couldn't quite taste its edgy momentary sweetness like sunrise fingering a young plant, like well water cooling a tin cup. He sensed forces set to make use of him, that wanted him harnessed to their needs, responsive to a few simple commands. Paid off in spare change and stale beer and hard laughs.

IT SEEMED LIKE CLOWNS WERE ALWAYS at an awkward stage. They no sooner tossed their caps in the air to graduate, when they found the next ladder, and set foot on its slippery bottom rung—or top rung at submarine school or mining college. That clownish misfit feeling, skating its sketchy dance moves, hiding its twitchy flat feet in big shoes, signalled a life pulling out of the station, huffing mixed metaphors, shouting all aboard.

THERE WAS NOTHING FUNNY ABOUT HER but the wink that might mean anything. Yet she startled the clown, made him bubble like a tar pit of slow laughter. Made him flush and spill his coffee. Made his fingertips itch, his hair tingle at the roots. Made him lose track of everything but the door she'd walked out and left open, letting all the biting cold life out there rush in and smack him.

WAS SHE A GIFT OR A SEDUCTION, or a way to skirt despair? Together they courted the heart's bonfire and ashen oblivion before they even knew who they were. What did she most want of him, and what did he most want of her? Their mutual excitement was its own excuse, its own reward, however it picked up and dropped them. The clown had no notion how much was at stake, what this first love might be costing. He had to admit the impulse that had hold of him was an overpowering way to insure the species ongoing. But the game was rigged—it drew them into itself, met its needs, then was done.

THOUGH HE KNEW WHICH FORK TO USE, the clown's social standing had always been awkward at best. To those with money and position he appeared rough around the edges, like any minute he might say or do something shaggy as his unkempt head. Which in some clown moods he did. But what was a haircut anyhow? A momentary attempt at neatening, that at best bespoke a sculptor armed with comb and scissors. When his country grandfather's haircut was botched by his surgeon son-in-law, the old man said that there wasn't but two weeks' difference between the best haircut and the worst. So was a haircut like cooking a pot roast, another immediate and modest act of love raised by its acceptance to an art?

HE STILL WAS ENTIRELY TOO SERIOUS. This late in his teens the most offensive name he could think of to call another to his face or behind his back was clown. Because the great offense was not to take yourself and your work and others seriously. To live for laughs. As a surrogate parent then a real parent, he was prey to that earnest self-regard and self-critique that clowns somehow avoided. Not that clowns weren't by and large full of themselves, inflated with pride, given to pranks and blind rages. But they were mostly not in earnest, which helped them cope with an indifferent, sarcastic, even cynical world, spackle over hard lumps, play along on what might as well be a brick trampoline, for all the give they felt.

AND EARNESTNESS COULD FEEL WORSE than clownery. The head and heart couldn't stand the battering without an occasional glancing blow from a rubber toy, a gentle pelting rain of rotten fruit.

THE CLOWN'S DAD WANTED HIM TO BE a doctor too, and for several years lobbied him with a fierce and charming impatience that was irresistible. Given a great and crushing gift, the boy scrubbed in and assisted at 37 major operations and countless minor procedures. He learned fast, watched and listened, kept his mouth shut, learned to anticipate and pass the right tools, hold clamps and retractors, drill holes in heads, witness and admire his father's matchless surgical skills. But finally it was no use. When any of his children wanted to talk to him after a long day, he'd growl What's your problem, as if that were all it could be, more of his life-and-death business. Then one day they summoned him and his son fresh out of surgery to the emergency room, to an eight-month-old baby girl. The baby and her young parents had been in a car crash, one of them already dead in the next room. The team worked swiftly and surely, had on hand the latest equipment. They drained a hematoma, opened a flap of skin to lift part of her skull, to relieve the pressure. They gave her blood and oxygen. And when her heart stopped they opened her chest to massage her tiny heart between gloved fingers. But the insult was too great, the life too slight and fresh. Nothing could have saved her.

FLUNKED OUT, WHEN HE TRIED TO GET BACK into college he was given an aptitude test. He answered each question as best he could, since he wanted to know what to do with his life more than they did. He'd taken a test few months before for the Air Force recruiter, where he'd gotten a perfect score. The recruiter had taken him in back and talked him out of enlisting, said it would be a waste. These test results favored law enforcement, journalism, social work. There was no hint of teaching or writing as careers. Which for a while led him to study Testing itself, since its façade hid clues to feeling's whereabouts. Which in turn led to the mother lode, Abnormal Psych.

THEN ALL AT ONCE THE CLOWN COUPLE were tossing out names for their new baby due any minute. They sensed this might be the dawn of their little world, the start of a grand opening. This morning she suggested Baxter—after the Jack Lemmon character in that classic movie with Shirley McLane. They agreed the name would be just odd enough and surely temporary, since the day would soon come when the kid would crave to hide behind an ordinary name. But to start the baby could be Baxter Jane, or Baxter Bob.

LATE ONE DAY THE CLOWN DROVE OUT with his beekeeper buddy to round up another swarm. They snipped the pulsing furry gold thing out of a lilac bush in some folks' yard, eased it into a garbage can, tied down the lid, gently set it in the trunk of the car, then wedged the can so it wouldn't flop around. It was like handling sweaty old dynamite without gloves. You didn't want to stir it up or bang it even lightly. You could feel the can vibrating, fanning itself like a giant fuzzy brain on overload. It was like the swarm was working on a problem you had no clue about, too busy to be bothered what you did. Then a couple miles toward home in the gathering dark his friend said Take the wheel, would you, pull over anywhere. He was already pulling down his pants and easing out the door when the clown stabbed the brakes, brought the car to a halt on the shoulder. Bees had crawled down inside his shirt and up his pants legs. The clown held the flashlight while his friend dropped his shorts, brushed and plucked them away with his fingertips. He said they must have liked him since they didn't sting him much.

THE CLOWN SAVORED THAT CALM in his voice. The beekeeper had once seen a horse kick over a beehive and get stung to death. Theirs was a force to be met with slow quiet moves, with a show of confidence and respect.

WHAT WAS HE DOING WHEN JFK WAS SHOT? He was in an Intro to Logic class in McMicken Hall, interrupted by wailing from the corridor. The professor dismissed the class, and he walked home to hold his nine-week-old baby daughter for the next four days, watching ghostly footage of a young president the same age as his dad, poised and jaunty, strong yet fragile, riding a whirlwind of change. Watching the nightmare parade through a black-and-white blizzard on TV, he fed her and played with her, held her even while she slept. There was no waking her to what this was about, why they were tearful and silent, why grownups welcomed her slight squirmy presence, waiting as they did for things to settle, the world to wake sane and calm. Some day he'd admit to her that didn't happen for another dozen years, past MLK and Bobby and Watergate, and still felt like something larger than any one man's toppling. Meanwhile her little life was up at all hours, flailing in the air, kicking off covers, offering the only hope there was.

THE YOUNG CLOWN'S WIFE GOT A JOB as a receptionist at a convalescent hospital for battered and tortured kids. It couldn't help but be a showplace of horrors, of stories nobody wanted to hear, or if you heard never repeated. The criminal perps were mostly parents and family, the children mostly too young to remember what had been done to them, or by whom. So on supervised visits their broken burned bodies still ached to be held by these monsters, and when the monsters were led away, the little ones were left, all tears and longing, inconsolable.

ONE SUNDAY MORNING HIS BABY DAUGHTER got into a dangerous pickle. She was keeping quiet in her crib because the big people were still asleep, but she was hungry and there was only one thing she could reach through the bars—a pack of cigarettes. She carefully took all the cigarettes out and one by one pulled the filters off and made a pile of them, then shucked the papers off the tobacco, made a neat pile of the papers, and started to eat the tobacco. It was sweet, since they used sugar to flavor the smoke and help stick it together. But it made her dangerously woozy. When her dad found her she was confused and feverish, so he called the doctor. And he said to get some ice cream and mush it up with cod liver oil, and feed her as much as she'd eat. Then watch her close. And for a while expect her diapers to be putrid.

THE CLOWN NOTICED IT WAS EASIER to feel clownish and behave clownishly when he drank. But it made no sense, taking the same medicine for sadness as for joy. It was only by not drinking at all for a while that he regained, however humbled and damaged, a lost sense of himself. Several times he quit for over a year, then had two beers to rub together, and next morning felt a little rough patch, a resistance to flow, to ready thought and action like barnacles on a boat. He had few heroes who had never touched a drop. He had one bright friend who even admitted he drank for the hangovers that shamed him back to work. Somewhere Milton had said he who would be an epic poet should drink only water from a wooden bowl. What was this love of the sauce that so distracted and disabled them, mangled and squandered them? A splash or two might make him sociable, but also made him start to feel rudderless, naked to invisible forces that spun and dropped him, till soon he was laughing at the spectacle of his own ruin, circling the maelstrom within a toilet bowl.

ONE EFFECT OF THE BOOZE was the delusion that he was funny. Others at the party took turns being hilarious, and once in a while one might become a barking scream. But a handful of them so medicated could get loud enough to drown out all objections. He knew it was hard to be funny, hard to get started, still harder to sustain. Like a sideshow act, like throwing knives blindfolded at a spinning target, drinking summoned mirages only to melt them, loosened the bracelets on his workaday self but kept them handy for later should he feel like boxing lessons, or caught a whiff of regret and went to throw it off the balcony.

HE CONSIDERED HIMSELF LUCKY to get sick before he got dead drunk. It meant his body knew a poison when it met one, tried to purge and save itself. Which going forward could be an edge for the species, or a throwback, depending. But it meant he never had blackouts, recalled in painful detail most of the stupid things said and done, as if some hijacker had bound and gagged the pilot but forgot the blindfold and earplugs. He recalled being carried up two flights of stairs over a friend's shoulder, tossed on the bed like a sack of spuds, with his sweatshirt on backwards, the big wet patch between his shoulder blades where he'd puked a whole bottle of bourbon, that someone had tried to clean off, then put back on him.

REGARDING HIMSELF IN THE MIRROR, the clown drunk raised a glass to the glass. A wave washed over, threatened to roll him, then its wavelets returning eased him out from the dock of himself. He shrugged. That was not him anymore, but so what. Here was the beauty of the solvent, that turned you into a stone baby, turned living inside out. For the moment the world was liquid and he was a sturdy but leaky boat, full to the gunnels, to the ear holes and eye holes and gob hole. His eyes were wet but his pants still dry for the moment. If he spilled out he wouldn't feel a thing—it would only mean a laugh.

ONE EVENING THESE TWO CLOWNS were drinking like they meant it, hard and fast. They'd taken the baby girl to the zoo that day, and of all the animals the ones that struck them most were an exhibit of transparencies: glass catfish and glass shrimp, window-pane bugs and beetles. You could see right through them, they were that obvious. It seemed there might be no lying in their world, where others could read your excitements, your bulldozed poker hands, empty pockets, over-drafts. They might see you were hungry, or what you'd been eating, they could tell if your liver was inflamed, your brain swollen. As with humans, the naked creature was an easy read. In order to deceive you put on clothes.

ARGUING WITH HIS DRUNKEN FATHER far into the night was for the young clown an endless source of fly-bys, of moths colliding softly under a feeble porch light. The young clown loved to speak of the mind, how it played with, sorted and ranked what it knew, how easily it disguised or confused what it looked at, how it even made up words to kid itself, tossed out fireworks like off your rocker or a bubble out of plumb. Which the old clown answered with his talk of brain mechanics, of synapses, wiring and juices, of stimuli and feedback loops, of quantum leaps and entropy, of chemistry and physics. Which made the sleepy young clown think of the brain as a gaudy bucket of goop with a ladle, that the old clown would use to scoop up the silver trout of thought before it jumped out on the floor.

BUT THEN TOO WHEN DRUNK the old man would blurt out nasty unanswerable things, and laugh at the effect, treat that sudden splash of cruelty like an object lesson for the young clown, that the world might never teach him otherwise. He would remark savagely on his son's appearance and prospects, mock a halting turn of phrase, a deferential delivery. And as the years went by, as the drink got a firmer seat in the saddle, the monster would appear earlier and stay later, with the stamina to outlast any sober affection or piety.

THE CLOWN'S DAD IN HIS CUPS liked to say there were too many chiefs and not enough Indians. And since he enjoyed giving orders, it was clear where he stood. Unexpectedly he'd growl "Stay out of the act" at his kids, make as if to backhand them, as if whatever he did at the moment were part of a vaudeville show in front of a live audience. Over the years the clown found other shy people who used anger to clear a path for themselves, to seize and hold the spotlight, though it was a bad habit to get into. The message to other clowns large and small was that the world had no room or use for them, that their role was mute obedience—that and wild applause.

ON THE OTHER HAND, CHILDREARING HAD its brushes with disaster even with him on duty. His baby daughter was fishing a silver earring out of the toaster with a fork when he looked up from feeding the new baby boy, and jumped to snatch her away. Sparks and miniature fireworks, and the toaster was history. The baby boy laughed but the little girl got serious a minute, scrunched her brow as he explained the danger of putting things in the toaster, especially metal things. But it was a measured warning. He didn't really want to frighten her. After all, at two and a half she could make her own toast and butter it.

THE CLOWN WAS TORN ABOUT fridge pictures and fridge magnets. That whole in-your-face temporary real estate that just kept growing till it fell off and stuck to the thing's metal ankles. There you confronted yourself while reaching for something cool, gratifying, refreshing. There it was, and there you were. Redolent not of the head and heart, but the belly. He recalled a fellow clown on a diet who hooked up a camera and switch on the fridge handle, to record every grand opening. The fridge front was an odd landing strip for kids' report cards and artwork, postcards with pithy quotes, photos of friends and relatives you'd otherwise never see. That you were forever reaching past to help yourself.

RECALLING SIGNS IN ODD PLACES, he had had a transmission installed in a shop with a big sign on the wall that said, "Shop Rate: $50 an hour—75 if you watch." And then there was the sign over his friend's dad's workbench, that said, "The hell it's yours—put it back." And the sign by the cash register in that friend's granddad's hardware store, that said "No credit to men with skinny mustaches." And there was the sign on the fridge in the break room of the car dealership that said "Eat your own lunch." Signs let you know where you stood.

THE SCHOLAR CLOWN KNEW that well before Shakespeare's day clown just meant a bumpkin, a rube, a plowboy or shepherd girl raised in the country, innocent of wicked city ways, attuned to a simpler life. Someone caught in the social fabric with no hope of rising, easily duped and fleeced, who got by with little show of ambition, never voicing secret hopes and dreams. For hundreds of years young farm clowns were drawn to the city, craving a life beyond subsistence, a roused ambition, a future. Shakespeare was once such a clown. So were Eli Whitney, Samuel Colt, Abe Lincoln, Henry Ford and Dwight Eisenhower. So were Frank and Jesse James.

FOR CENTURIES CLOWNS STOOD OUT at the edges of crowds, on the shoulders of roads. Timeless, irrelevant, impertinent. Country folks in outlandish clothes, each one of a kind all homespun, handwoven, cross-stitched, shaped to the body that bore them, shoes beat out on a last with

71

a cudgel, then by the foot in the furrow, hats never blocked or formed but by slapdash necessity, that gripped the skull anyhow, practically never blew away.

LIKEWISE NEITHER WAS A SCARECROW a suit of worn-out clothes stuffed with straw propped up to frighten thieves from any crop ripening. Crows didn't scare easy and loved to pick through a feast. So it was first and forever an otherwise useless ragged man made to stand guard in field and orchard, with stones in his pockets.

THE THING TO SUSPECT ABOUT SHAKESPEARE at 52 was that he didn't think he was done. He'd bought a cozy London nest, the gatehouse by Blackfriars, where the quills were sharpened, the ink fresh. In Stratford he was just getting things neatened up, taking his first real rest, when, as the story had it, his old rival Ben Jonson with fellow poet Michael Drayton came to town, looked him up, and insisted on a carouse for old time's sake. Whether the bumpers brought the fever or vice versa, he must have thought let that be a lesson. There is no drinking one's health.

THE CLOWN TRIED HARD TO SEE who Shakespeare was, through the mist and dust of the centuries, the glitter and glare of his plays. The richest girl in Stratford is wooed and won by an ambitious devious glove maker who deals in shady wool futures. Their most promising son marries early then runs off to the city, joins a troupe of players. There nearly everyone likes him, but for rivals who can't contain their jealousy toward one who scarce blotted a line. The clown thought everyone has a life, a growing-up story, but mostly not a story to be told head-on. And that upbringing must be gentle enough on the artist that broken bones heal and you're not just a maze of old scars crying out remembered pain. For art to bloom you have to know what you know and suspect what you suspect, work a pliable versatile medium, and since amusement is your game accept how you appear to others, not squander your life pointing fingers, naming names.

turning pro

"When the going gets weird, the weird turn pro."
                                         –Hunter S. Thompson

THE GRADUATE CLOWN NEEDED a fresh start—new places, new people, new work and play without dismissal or shame. So he piled in the car and headed West, to where the Sixties were in bloom, streets overrun with all manner of novelties. The unpopular and escalating war had been a well-kept secret where he was from. The fix had been in so long in that Midwest backwater that even the stagnation had a shine, the flash of fresh-printed money untouched by workaday hands. Here was a new world in the making, an eclectic romp across cultures and centuries that borrowed from everywhere to clothe and enlighten itself. That labored to create and honor its own music, refine its own language, forge and hone its beliefs. That tried to cobble whole communities out of illusory materials, drugs and jazz riffs, whiffs of incense and mirrors, with fresh customs conjured to ground them, fresh ethics. The only trouble was that everything needed fixing all at once. Everyone had to be heard, every possibility craved airing, and some of the most articulate and able were stunned into silence by conflicting overwhelming needs. Hope was fragile, easily co-opted, diverted by the rants of false messiahs, or stilled by a few well-aimed blows with a truncheon. So politics papered over failure, the next cause displaced the last one, lights flickered, the streets grew quiet, and in the dark the movement stumbled.

YET HIPPIES WENT FORTH DAILY IN COSTUME, in drag, in mufti. As with any clown parade it became an impromptu dance, a promenade that included touches of posing and swagger, though nothing unusual for the young. Reinventing oneself was the order of the day, and might invoke beards, flowing tresses, face paint and feathers, stripes and fringes, boots and sandals, outrageous flowered hats and patchwork vests, flags and furs worn for effect, pins and badges, honorary medals, brilliant sashes, sturdy belts. And in fair weather the perfect disguise—supple skintight skin itself.

TAKING TO THE STREETS IN PROTEST he felt like the eyes and ears of an endless long-suffering animal. Walking quietly he saw how he was seen by fellow citizens, both those marching with him and those stalled or pushed aside by this vast body moving slowly through their midst. Some self-styled organizers in costume chanted slogans, flaunted signs and banners, but the great bulk of the demonstration remained spontaneous and anonymous. Each pair of feet, hands, eyes working this Chinese paper dragon still counted for only one self. Some other players watching felt they owned the streets—merchants and property owners along the way, and police assigned to crowd control. Their riot gear without nametags and badge numbers let him know what frustrations lay just under the surface, what retaliation might appear once night fell, with news cameras packed up or chased off. After the speeches to expect a nightstick and tear gas finale.

WHEN YOU LOST EVERYTHING how did you find your way without even a trail of bread crumbs? He drove to Portland with friends to read poems and hang out. At the poetry reading that night they met friendly strangers, got invited to crash on the floor. And spent most of the night talking, then in the morning splashed water on their faces, piled back in the car to go to a school across the river in Vancouver, where one of them had a musical gig. On the way there he discovered his briefcase was not in the car. It was a sleek black indestructible fiberglass thing, a gift that held everything he'd ever written. He dropped his friends at the school, and headed straight back to Portland. He didn't know the names of the people or the street where they lived. He didn't know where to even start looking, only knew he'd last seen the case standing at the curb by the open trunk. His mind was reeling. His first thought was that the fancy new case would tempt thieves, who might just dump his poems and stories out in some dumpster or trash can. Why hadn't he just used a brown paper bag? Then he thought someone might keep everything to sort through later, but he didn't think his name and address were anywhere inside the thing, so it would be useless to post a reward. Finally came the worst thought, that whoever took the case might keep only the best pieces, to pass off as his own, and throw out the rest. Which dragged him back around to that first nightmare thought of the dumpster. As he neared the Southwest side of town he willed himself to be calm, told himself just mirror the turns he'd made to get on the freeway. When four or five turns later he pulled up to the house where they'd crashed, there was the case where he'd left it, wet with rain, still on the sidewalk untouched.

THE CLOWN HAD JUST GOTTEN A MANDOLIN, and after spending long nights and weekends playing every tune he could halfway remember, he went to a music party. The easy part was the tune. The hard part was the timing, the playing along, fitting in. That night there was a man he'd heard on the radio, a late-night DJ. He hadn't known the man was a musician. Or that he couldn't see. That night the blind DJ played every instrument at the party—piano, dulcimer, accordion, guitar, fiddle, saxophone, clarinet, mandolin, drums, standup bass, flute, harmonica—everything. Not to show off, the group of them were just trading instruments, and as each in turn came around to him it was like greeting an old friend. He could tune each for himself, could lead and follow, had the musician's deference and decorum down. That night the clown started playing in the dark, quit looking at his hands, started listening to these sound boxes held close in the night as a lover, felt how each made something else in him sing, offered another throat and voice, another heart and lungs.

DRIVING WEST THE LITTLE GIRL CLOWN persuaded her tiny brother to throw his empty milk and juice bottles out the window when the grownups weren't looking. The only signs were an uncommon neat-ness, and muffled giggling. When they stopped for lunch there would be no bottles to rinse and refill. It took a while to catch the signal passed between the two tiny mugs when they thought the coast was clear, then see the milk splash on the highway behind them. It might be a tad early, but was time for that talk on recycling.

IT WAS NOON WHEN THEY PULLED INTO Rawlins, that he recalled from his drive back from California at 4. The town then had had real cowboys, saddled horses tied to hitching posts. There was none of that anymore, though a Chinese restaurant on the main drag looked faded and dusty enough to have been going back then, so he pulled over. Told the kids and their mom he'd be just be a minute, needed to check something first. Then he went in, dazed from days on the road, ap-proached the waitress and tried to frame his need. He said Could you ask the cook to step out of the kitchen, please? She studied his crazy smile, saw no danger, walked to the back and spoke to the cook. Out stepped a Chinese man who when the clown waved smiled and waved back. So here might be real Chinese food.

HE TOOK THE LITTLE ONES to a Rock Festival & Lighter-Than-Air Fair, brought chips and pop and sun lotion, even steaks and charcoal, but forgot a grill or pan and utensils. Luckily he had a pocketknife. So after sunset between bands he went to a garbage barrel, dug out some empty tin cans, smashed them flat, tore off the labels. Then scraped a pit, made a fire, and when it died down layered tin cans over the coals, got them glowing like metal shingles, then tossed on the steaks. When they were done he cut the meat in chunks and strips that they ate with their fingers, passed around on a plank.

ONE GRAY WINTER DAY IN 1969 he went to SeaTac Airport to pick up a friend whose flight was delayed. While he sat by the gate he fingered an ashtray filled to overflowing with Army medals and patches. Someone had cut or torn away every official sign from his uniform, down to the eagle shirt-buttons. Gone all his experience, honors, name, rank, identity. It was a gesture of erasure for some survivor, a near-suicide, the only answer he could make to a homecoming of rejection, anger, despair, home from an arrogant, deceitful, unwinnable war.

AT FIRST HIS FOOLISHNESS WAS UNCONSCIOUS, a warty excrescence or cowlick, a giggle in church for the uncle who sat on his hat, a gush of the life force that couldn't help itself. Then for a while the silly excesses would surprise his serious self, no telling when and where one might surface, derail the ostensible grownup. Till at last something in him came to prize this foolery, even plan for it. Jokes and juggling, verses of songs and dance moves. Your Red Scarf Matches Your Eyes, all matters of timing rehearsed till he sensed the perfect spot, the still pool that begged for a belly flop.

BUT THEN TOO SOMETIMES THAT CLOWN FEELING stiffened, held tight, froze for days, months, crank parades of years. There was that humorless stretch when the bottom fell out of his world, first the twin assassinations of Martin and Bobby that bled like open wounds, then a sham party convention where people in the Chicago streets chanted "The whole world's watching!" while cops swinging clubs waded in. With shameless maneuvers around this crucial election, all he'd hoped for vanished, turned and ran. In the end he sat alone in a bar watching election returns, as a long-haired wild man came in, a latterday prophet in a patchwork vest, shouting I voted for the Antichrist, bring on the night! And with Nixon pledging peace but delivering war down it came.

HE KNEW VAGUELY SOME DAYS HE FELT irresistible, some days anything but. It was a matter of timing, maybe the phase of the moon, maybe who he reminded someone of, not what he wore, how he looked. But on some days the girls and women beamed and nodded, even kids waved as he passed. He knew he wasn't all that charming, and such days might be rare, but when it happened he felt like a clown in a parade of one, walking along doing imaginary tricks one after another—juggling oranges, playing a herky-jerky march on the guitar, flipping his hat in the air and catching it on his noggin.

HE GREW A BIG RED BEARD that covered six or seven years and half of Iowa, halfway to his belly button. That let everyone know he was grown up, that like Whitman said, "These are the days that must happen to you." It told flirty girls to back off, he had things to do besides shave. But it was a hideout, just like his big red nose would be later on, his shiny head, baggy clothes, floppy shoes. When kids said he had crumbs in his beard, he'd say That's the mouse's dinner, point up under his chin where it lived, watch them stare. Then he cut it off, hacked and scraped for hours, surprised how naked and cold his face felt, how every little gust he caught square on the chin spun him like a weather vane. How tender and thin his skin stayed under all that thicket like a baby animal, how profusely it bled when touched wrong.

THE DOWNTURN PAST CLOWNERY CAME when he lived among people who would be on the outside forever. In ghettos, basements, in hideouts with no street address, on the edges, in high weeds at the end of unpaved roads turned to gravy in a drizzle. Folks who knew the official world would never come knocking to help them, who got by on their wits best they could, without help from landlords or employers who'd work them without mercy off the books, who if they got sick lost a paycheck if not heart, mind, hope. A few of these preyed on each other, some congratulated themselves on figuring how to prey on the strong, but many got a job and made a life of belt-tightening at hard labor with no vacations, short rest, the rare smoke break a cynical death-wish. Any distant residual hope resided in their young, who out of a crackling static-charged despair might blunder into being, in a moonlit moment flourish, in spite of the neatly stacked odds.

THE BABY GOATS WERE UP ON THE ROOF of the trailer, and no one slept a wink for their crying, their hoofbeat clatter on the aluminum like dumptruck gravel. Who could blame them—there were hungry coyotes and wild dogs in these dark hills, so they wouldn't jump down until daybreak. They needed a billy goat to do battle and stand guard, though that might be even worse for the humans and their babies lying exhausted inside, as bad as the shotgun with a flashlight taped to the barrel, that had so far been tested and failed.

IN SECOND GRADE HIS BRIGHT LOVELY DAUGHTER mastered the Knowing Question, which she would bring home and deliver fearlessly. This was her first year in a regular button-down school, so he knew where it came from. She'd say Dad, are we rich or poor? She might ask, Are we hippies? And yet another time, Why don't we go to church? She wouldn't pile them on, just lay one out and patiently wait for his answer. He knew better than try to deflect her with questions of his own. Other kids went from open-range innocence to caged adulthood without ever uttering such things out loud. The girl's clown parents were still young, so the answers at least felt original—though for all the serious intent sometimes laughable. But better this than the kind of talk that ended with one big voice shouting None of your beeswax!

THE CLOWN STUDIED HERMIT CRAB DISGUISES, how they scuttled naked in the shallows from one borrowed shell that pinched to a new one a size or two larger, that might be grown into, worn awhile. Like families at spring cleaning, passing around their hand-me-downs.

Then there were snakes in spring shedding last year's skin, somehow scraping and wiggling free, a one-piece striptease marvelous even out to the lidless eyes. And the trees widening their stance and girth, straining and splitting their bark to reach every which way. The lesson grow or die. Even rooted in place here no staying the same, staying put.

THAT SUMMER HIS FATHER CAME WEST for a whirlwind visit, just one night, and brought along the whole gang of young ones left at home. So the clown set up the barbecue, lit coals and grilled them all dinner. When they'd finished their hamburgers and hot dogs, baked beans, chips and ice cream and pop, the young ones going fishing tomorrow went to bed at the hotel eight or nine blocks away, while the clown and his dad settled in to drink and talk. The father's disappointment and anger were palpable. The clown had a summer job driving truck for a cardboard box company, but his life seemed a mess. Alone, broke and desperate, he was still reading and writing every spare moment. When it got late and time to go, the clown worried his dad might get lost on the streets, so offered to walk him home. Off they went, still chafing, each feeling misunderstood, saying the other had no idea what he was about. His father was still young enough to plan to wear him down, outdrink and outlast him. But the clown got tired of being called a sorry drifter, and countered by saying his dad had never known a real artist. As for teaching, he told his father he was brilliant but not patient enough with mistakes to value a student's accomplishments. When they arrived at the hotel they were still burning a lit fuse a ways from the dynamite, so his father said he would walk him home, and that was that. So they set out, but met the same result back at the clown's house, and avoided the inevitable goodbye, going round the dark streets back and forth. They hadn't drunk enough to just shout the same things over and over, but there was a common thread. His father had always wanted the clown to follow in his footsteps, and when he heard the boy wanted to write and teach, his father said he was condemning himself to a life of poverty and irrelevance. That whole night passed in their to and fro, four or five times around, but somewhere in there the talk got a little sweeter, less judgmental parent and defiant child. Somewhere stumbling the dark leafy streets with the wind sighing through them they reached some agreement. As if there were a truth that needed those dark miles walked alongside the other to accept who was walking who home, and who had to live apart. And no more damn silence. There was light in the east when the clown laid down for twenty minutes with all his clothes on. He had a low-wage rendezvous with a truck and loading dock downtown at six o'clock sharp.

THIS CIRCUS CLOWN FELL IN LOVE with an elephant. More precisely he fell in love with every grand thing about her, her 300 pounds of hay a day, her crazed baggy suit, her mountainous poop, her hawser-firehose nose that could pluck and shuck a lone peanut. He especially loved how, when they'd chain her in place by one ankle, swaying side to side she'd put herself deep in a trance, levitate and depart. His heart was taken with her vast pure substantial intelligence, that remained fleeting and delicate. At first he couldn't tell and didn't even care if she loved him back.

THE SIGN ON HER CAGE said Jasmine, but that couldn't be her name in Elephant. He wondered what he should call her, what her real name could be, did she even have a name. Maybe her name was an ancient rumble of pleasure and warning in her mother's throat. What did she call herself? No wonder she mostly didn't answer when he spoke. So like all true lovers at last the clown greeted her saying only Hey You, in her presence feeling his eggshell words drop and break.

THEY WORKED UP AN ACT he called the Statue. He led her into the ring, sometimes painted pink if there was time for the messy scrubdown after. Then he went into his drunk act, usually the one full of oblivious happiness but not always, staggering, leaning against her as he tried to tie a shoelace that squirmed and threatened to crawl off. At his signal, finger to lips, she would stand in place while he did the act around her. A clown cop would come by, and a clown lady of the evening. He would try to whistle at the girl, but would fail to make a sound. So the elephant would raise her trunk and the band would blow a foghorn. He loved how the elephant was invisible to everyone but him. How the girl clown found him irresistible, though she was a head taller and too wide to see around. How the clown cop would go to arrest him, but the elephant would stick out her trunk, and he'd be knocked out by her breath. She could stand forever, hold still for him no matter what petty mayhem swirled around them. And after the applause, the bows, backstage he would bow again, and turn out his peanut pockets to thank her.

*THE CLOWN DREAMT OF HELPING HER ESCAPE, slipping away
some foggy night and hiding in the woods till the circus moved on and the
sheriff quit looking. But that was impossible. Her very non-belonging in a
thicket would make her obvious. Besides, what would she eat while they hid?
He wished he could afford to keep an elephant—though come to think of it,
having just one would be cruel. He knew she was lonely, that she wanted the
whole herd within reach of her trunk, her family grazing a wide savanna
where but for monsoon season it might rain a little every other day, with riv-
ers, mud wallows, dung beetles, the warm pungent land of her dreams.*

*EVEN CLOWNS OUTGROW THE CIRCUS but in the end he couldn't
leave her, so they grew old together, playing Hide-the-Peanut and other silly
wordless games. He donated half his pay to meet her feed bills, got so he'd
only work with her and she with him, which if he couldn't find her another
elephant became more or less like a marriage. And slept in the straw in her
cage, where they snored lightly together.*

THE CLOWN CRAVED TO SLEEP like he slept as a boy, in dreams
of flying over his everyday life from on high. With gentle fingertip
motions he would soar and weave through obstacles, with a roll of his
hips and shoulders squeak past treetops, tip his head and tuck his chin
to swoop near anything he craved to see. It was swimming in air, as
effortless as fish and birds. His flight powered and controlled by will,
by modest shifts in attention, by pure curiosity, warping his wings like
a Wright Brothers' biplane, so subtle and flexible, with no engine, no
exhaust, with but a whispering wind in his ears. The air was dense and
sustained him, yet was crystal-clear. To wake, all he had to do was touch
down, with no fear of falling, no hard landings in a world doughy-soft
everywhere.

BUT IN HIS EXISTENTIAL DREAM these nights the clown wan-
dered edges, along dry mountain trails sloughed away, buried in rubble,
forgotten. In these steep hidden valleys with no outlooks, no warning
signs, he had to watch every barefoot step, beyond hope of reckoning.
The days were all the same, blazing and myopic, and one morning he
slipped and dropped off, woke to find himself bruised and wedged in
a steep-walled crevasse with no escape. But then groping in shadows
he found a faint trail leading downhill through a cave, dropping out of
confinement, emptying the bottom of despair. The way led over rock,

with not a footprint or claw mark showing anyone had come this way before. Winding down the way opened out in green vistas at last, where he found himself chuckling and whistling, at this way untouched by any other life spent lost, footloose, at odds, made not by some flimsy intelligence, but carved just so by wind and water.

HE DREAMT TOO OF BEING IN PRISON, where the one comfort in his cell was a rocker, that didn't squeak a bit on the painted concrete floor. Once a month a lovely friend would come visit him. She was never in a hurry, always seemed genuinely glad to see him, spoke lightly and clearly of magical things she'd seen and done outside his walls. Still, she didn't smile like she used to. He sensed it was getting harder to manage these visitations alongside the rest of her life. He dreamt he rocked all the while she wasn't there, reading silently, playing music softly to himself, sometimes even sleeping in motion. But when she came he couldn't sit still, was always up and moving, though the guards would sometimes shout Sit down, loud enough to wake him.

THEN ONE NIGHT HE DREAMT a grand parade with a first row all skinny long-legged clowns with big feet, not marching exactly, doing a shuffling quickstep that went sideways and backwards and every which way. No thought to where they were going, just leaned way way back, highstepping and sidestepping down the street, followed by bands and floats, baton-twirlers in spangles. With golden palominos prancing, shaking out their flowing manes and tails, and other clowns with brooms and shovels making a dance of the cleanup. Just then he recalled what the skinny clowns up front were doing—a cakewalk! That looked like fun, so he jumped up and ran after. But they were too big and too limber, stepping too fast and too slow. His own feet worked like drowsy grasshoppers, too lazy to catch the beat, and there was no cake anyhow, they'd already eaten every crumb.

THIS YOUNG MAN HAD A FAVORITE UNCLE Fred, who'd been a clown till he died, and had no family, no kids, so the boy got all his stuff— the makeup tacklebox, some red fringe bald wigs and fright wigs, bowler hats, great long sighing shoes that nattered like ducks when you cantered, baggy pants and suspenders, a teeny green jacket, bow ties that lit up, smoked and twirled. So he thought maybe sometimes he should dress up, do his uncle's old act. Who would mind? What could it hurt? That first Halloween, he went to a couple parties where everyone laughed at his footwork, and squeezed his red nose for luck. So he started going to the hospital, to the kids' ward, where Fred had volunteered. His uncle had taught him how to make balloon weenie dogs, swords and snake hats and whatnot. And at the hospital right away they called him Sorry Fred, which was his uncle's clown name. Maybe they didn't know the difference. One could hope.

IT WAS GOOD HE HAD ALL FRED'S EQUIPMENT. Even with wet fingers stuck in light sockets, some clown hair refused to stick up. Which explained the brisk sale in wiggery. Some sagging frowny faces called for a big painted smile and vice versa. One's appearance was meant to signal momentary doubts, confusion, lostness, the difficulty of trudging in size 22 feet when your heart felt a waltz coming on.

SORRY FRED HIS UNCLE DID SOME TRICKS so old no one knew where they came from, even what to call them, that the nephew couldn't touch. When Fred had performed them no telling should they laugh or weep. He could mesmerize a chicken, lay her back along one arm, stroke her under the chin while he chicken-talked and yodeled till she went limp, had to be revived with a magic word and a pinch of the cornmeal she favored. He could do back-country clogs and jigs, fancy footwork that only came to him in the right setting, a hoedown or barn dance where his elbows would start pumping while his feet squeaked and slapped on the boards. Cantering along he could lean way back, kick off his hat from behind, then leap up and catch it. And as a finale, he could stumble-step his bowler hat from one outstretched hand to the other across his whole wingspan, then walk it halfway back, hunch his shoulders and tip it up on his head. And when he took a bow the hat would raise up all by itself.

HE KNEW WEARING HIS UNCLE'S FRIGHT WIG, tattered pants and noisy shoes disguised his own fitness and youth. The makeup hid his eyes and mouth behind his uncle's sad yet maddening mug. From watching other clowns he knew his juggling and music and acrobatics would just get better with age. Likewise his birdcalls, his blinking and lying, his stuttering doubletalk. His brazen erasure of the obvious ran counter to what many old people did—dyeing their hair, shining their dentures, hiring surgeons to nip and tuck their sags and bulges, anything to play young. He figured he'd keep in practice, though getting old might take forever at this rate.

83

THE YOUNG ACTOR CLOWN WAS SCARED to death to perform, so froze in tortured attitudes. Yet something in him was deeply stirred by the chance of public failure. The transparent guise of himself in a play that was not him nor about him grabbed his total attention. And the lockstep of learning lines and moves as if marching in boot camp. Along the way he realized that though the audience could see these were actors pretending, they couldn't quite see into him. Mostly they saw the costume, the outsides, the ant-mine sugar frosting of the lame act he put on. They couldn't see into his feelings, what drove and moved him, what flexed the fist in the puppet. So for performance he needed to summon a taste of the real thing, know which pocket that feeling was tucked in, get it wound up and cocked, like a jack-in-the box set to spring.

IN HER TINY APARTMENT THE TWO OLD LADIES were going through their dead mother's things. Giving away to this young family the overstuffed chair where they both did their homework as girls. Dangled their legs reading listening to the radio. Gently insisting on what these young folks might need, especially the big red-handled fork that one of the daughters had given her mother and sister. So all three had used the same one to cook the same things, baked chicken and turkey and pot roast, that the clown accepted like he'd been given a live human heart with a comfortable handle.

THE CLOWN FOUND A STORE that sold Wild Card Ice Cream for 99 cents a half-gallon. Plain cartons that held all different colors and flavors, no two identical. For years he would buy it, and the kids and their friends were amused enough to eat it. They only had to throw away one carton so ugly nobody would touch. Years later he took students on a tour of the ice cream plant where the Wild Card flavors had come from, found out that this was how they'd clean out the lines between mixing different batches, that would push out a few gallons of odd colors and flavors without rhyme or reason. Strawberry ice cream tinted green, chocolate chip mint colored red, purple peach, on and on.

HE WAS DRIVING THROUGH REDWOODS, from Grant's Pass west on 199 out to the coast. It was late night, they'd been on the road since Seattle, and Jack's headlight switch on the old Valiant station wagon was wobbly, sparking and treacherous. Jack had been driving it like this, with a popsicle stick whittled to wedge the shaft, since the year before. He'd been a bomber pilot in WWII, had made it back from turning German cities to cratered moonscapes and char. Some might call this part of his fatalistic lucky style, but it was truly something else. At the wheel the clown would dive into each turn, memorize a snatch of road, then the lights would die, leave them black on black under giant trees shut overhead, bereft of moon and stars. He'd steer while jiggling the switch till it came back on, showed where they'd been in the meantime, more or less. He slowed way down but there was no flashlight in the car, no one else on the road to lead or follow, no sniffing out the way except to scour the gravel shoulders. In one of the headlight flickers he noticed Jack had his door cracked, set to bail with no chute. After hours of this they wound down out of the hills into Crescent City, where both of them took a breath. Jack said How could you do that? He said How could you right back. Next morning when the car parts place opened he was there buying Jack a new switch, that he put in before he would hand back the keys.

HIS TWO SMART SILLY KIDS HAD A CAT who would eat lima beans and other foods they didn't care for, that were supposedly good for them, smuggled in a napkin to her under the table. She was known to have eaten mushrooms, tomatoes, creamed corn—the list went on and on. No rare gormandizing feline, Emily didn't like such grub any more than little clowns did, but she was so sure of their affection she accepted what was offered, and did what she was told. At the time there seemed no greater love, as if from a fellow jailbird.

HE ADMIRED EXCEPTIONAL ANIMALS. The sheep dog that knew the thousand words naming his toys. Ravens and crows and parrots raised by hand that bonded with humans for life, that mimicked their laughter and accents. But he'd also known hogs that ran hog-wild, met cheerful raccoon babies that grew into savages bent on destruction when their brains grew too tight for their skulls. He cheered the White Whale that rammed the Essex and Pequod, and savored Odysseus' old dog Argos on the dung heap who after an eternity raised his head, saw through his master's disguise, and wagged his tail.

85

AT THE ZOO THE LITTLE GIRL MONKEY had only one arm, but she could still be a swinger since she was a New World monkey with a prehensile tail. The boy monkey was fast but knew not to get too far ahead, maybe give her half a chance at his secret game. He'd snatched a glass slide off the table through the bars unbeknownst to the clown in the lab coat. He was hiding it in his mouth, leading the girl monkey on a breathless aerobatic chase. When she'd tire, he'd stop, and behind the clown's back make as if to let her touch it. Reach out and offer a taste. They had no clue what the slide was about, just knew it belonged to the jailers and tasted funny. It couldn't be good for jailed monkeys, but was small, mysterious, near invisible, perfect for their sport.

THIS CLOWN HAD AN AFRICAN GREY PARROT that could talk. In no particular order Butch would shout Hook Me Up, My Bad, It's All Good, Absolutely, and You Gotta Be Kidding Me! No questions, no doubts, the perfect running commentary—though the owner hadn't realized he'd be stuck with his smartass teen self for the next twenty years, with no more melody than a buzzard, no more thought than a chickadee. He knew the parrot had no clue what he was saying. But Butch was observant, could read the clown's moods, and either had comic timing or a razor sense of irony.

THE WRITER CLOWN WONDERED WHAT was the highest praise you could give a book. In truth that might be "I wish I'd written this, but since you did, I feel relieved I don't have to." Which might sound like laziness, but was anything but. And much finer than raw jealousy. It was nice to admit he might not have done half the job before his pencil pooped out or snapped.

HE KNEW WHAT HE WANTED IN A BOOK—for it to trick him, not to get long in the tooth, not to go breathless and quit. Convince him it was made not of words, but of life. No matter how much or how often he read it—which for most books was not much, once or less plenty, though for a few once a year not enough—it shouldn't feel like a hospital visit, dutifully standing around trying not to stare at where it was hooked up to monitors and drips and nutrients, sucking away at the culture on life support. Which of course to live it had to be. But if the patient could be forgiven this being dead on arrival, given a chance of

survival though cobbled of words warped and rusty, left out in the rain
centuries, what he craved was to be with Huck Finn, haggling a catfish
open with a sawblade missing its handle, or in the muddy river up to his
chin watching the dawn coming on.

AND ALL AROUND HIM WERE STORIES kept chained up, that
leapt and slobbered to be written but so what. His next-door neighbor
was a portly ex-cop whose one ambition had been to be an opera singer.
Whose dad had warned him cops were lazy, on the take, afraid of honest
work. He lived in a tiny cottage with one bedroom and a pull-out bed
under the seat on the porch, had a wife with a job as bank teller, and a
bleach-blonde teenage daughter who slept late, dressed wild, snuck out
and ditched school, while he did odd jobs that let him sing at the wheel
of his highway patrol surplus cruiser, driving convoy for Wide Loads,
playing guard and night watchman. The cottage also housed Turkey,
his German shepherd who went along on guard jobs, otherwise barked
nonstop at whoever walked by, rattling their thin wooden walls. A tough
guy, when no one was watching he did his own dentistry with pliers.

OR HOW ABOUT THE OLD BOATBUILDER who lived uphill,
with his son, who had made wooden boats his whole life? Ran a boat-
yard that built tugs and fishing boats, sail and power pleasure boats, but
he wouldn't go out on the water, got seasick, in all his years never spent
a night aboard even one of his boats. When they christened a new one,
the yard crew had to trick him into joining the launch party. They'd ask
the boss to check something important aboard, then fire up the engine
and toss off the lines before he could hop off. He couldn't fire them for
wanting to have him along. And though miserable he also felt welcome,
in charge.

THEN THERE WERE HIS TWO LITTLE NEPHEWS who fig-
ured how to beat the new electronic pop machines—until their parents
caught them at it. Their four little hands would hover over the selec-
tion buttons like baby raccoons, and they would beat out a wild jungle
rhythm, up and down faster and faster, till the machine was stymied,
overcome and surrendered, and out rolled a cold can of pop. They were
heartbroken when their parents made them go inside the store and pay
for it. And worst of all, soon they couldn't even say what the trick had
been, how it worked.

AMONG LONGER FULLER STORIES, his country grandfather had been the most cosmopolitan, evenhanded, grounded human being he had known. By turns school teacher, storekeeper, farmer and county commissioner, with, as he put it, a finger in several other pies. Then years after the old man died, the clown craved to know the real man behind the quiet façade. So he went to the library, dug out the rolls of the 1880 Census, when his grandfather had been six years old, to see the world he'd grown up in. Of the 26,671 residents of that rural county then, a third were German, a third English, Scots and Irish, and the rest were French, Dutch, and other northern European nationalities. There was but one black family, nine souls at one address, all with the same last name. And there was exactly one of what the Census Taker termed a "chinaman"—poor lone soul. So much for ethnic diversity. So much for propinquity as the font of worldly wisdom. Then he recalled that as his grandfather aged he talked less. Spoke in riddles, brooked no easy answers. Softly said All men are brothers.

FROM ENDLESS LOVE STORIES HE LEARNED how marriage like life itself could be short, uncertain, bittersweet. Nothing paid enough to keep the wrong twosome together sixty-something years. But did you even know till you tried what kids these days blithely called a starter marriage? It was tricky. You could be faithful and attentive, passionate in bed, generous, hard-working, slow to anger, quick to forget and forgive, you could deliver the moon on a silver cheese platter, and still wake up forlorn as an Iowa cornfield. As for youth and beauty, bright surfaces reflected squarely in the eyes: sweets festered. Some couples didn't sing in the same key, or the same tune long, much less each others' tunes. Then too there was change, growing together or apart as the glaciers of opinion melted and absconded, or cooled and formed. Loving might begin as predilection, as built-in bias, but was also commitment, a persistent willingness to chip away at the mountain side by side, till something dawned bigger than both of you, that together you'd identify and name.

CLOWNS DIDN'T MAKE SUCH BAD PARENTS, since everyone could use help with their makeup and juggling. But there was a problem with clowns having kids. For their first growing years you were entirely immersed in what kept them well, what made them sick, how they slept, what they ate—you watched everything. So much that you had no time or mind for reflection, for the bigger issues until you met them in the hallway at first grade. Where you found yourself staring down the gun barrel of Education, what it meant for them and their future. Could this sorry world shape up, could it get better in time to make any difference? Your own chance may have flown, but these little ones' chance was right now, shaking the dust off their wings.

SUDDENLY HE WAS A SINGLE PARENT. Teenage kids could be clowns themselves, surely knew how it took one to know one, but then they needed a dad to be stable and in charge, predictable, even boring. Someone who worried late, slept fitfully, rose early, and kept the porch light on. Otherwise someone whose life was work. Luckily the women who used to be in his life were still there around the edges, keeping an eye out for trouble, though they weren't right here where the parade was ongoing. Yet for all the partying, all the crash-and-burn, these bright youngsters of his were serious, only clowning off and on.

THE CLOWN'S FRIEND HAD BEEN an in-law who unlike the rest of the clan refused to divorce him when the moment came. The two of them carried their status as outlaws lightly, but the friend meant it deeply, like an old joke tried and true. A scientist, the friend expressed himself in a courtly and elegant manner, but always did things in his own quirky reasonable way. As a teenager he had started throwing himself a birthday feast, no gifts allowed, invited whoever he wanted, and paid for everything. As they aged, he was the final friend who would knock on his door every month or so out of the blue, without calling ahead like stupid busy grownups learn to do. So the friend sometimes got to watch him work, see certain secret clown doings done in the shop on the workbench. Even autopsies of things gone wrong. And mingling theory with practice, sometimes they would talk for hours while the clown gently sharpened his tools.

BY WAY OF ROMANCE HE LEARNED eventually that gratitude was a sorry excuse for seduction. As was pity. That youth was a flimsy disguise, and cuteness wore thin, your own and anyone else's. So what then could love be rooted in but mysterious sharings, affinities that might outlast that first insane rush, that feverish obliviousness, to become a habit of nakedness and vulnerability in the presence of the other, that stirred both awake at first light? Otherwise love was a spindly growth in shadows, a house plant soon to topple. Beyond which he considered how for all its physical alchemy love over time amounted to a friendship, so took work. You couldn't really keep score, that kind of counting meant death. Even if you said thanks and meant it, that was never enough. You had to try to give more than you got, to make up for those times you didn't notice or recall who really picked up the check, how that tasty pizza floated in at the perfect moment, landed only to be inhaled in mid-thought by those other faces glowing in the candlelight.

GOING OUT FOR THE EVENING he considered there might be people at the party who didn't play by any rules he knew, who changed games on a whim, who enjoyed taking advantage, damaging so-called friends, making reckless moves as a way of getting charged, raising the stakes to keep things interesting, yelling bloody murder while they snatched up whatever lay unattended. Such players felt a mighty urge to replace the duties and pleasures of life, all its predictable interactions, with spicy fierce games of one's own concoction. On the way out the door he looked in the little mirror, not to see if his face was on crooked, but to see should he really be going.

YET WHAT DID APPEARANCES MATTER? Like most clowns he had secrets he wore on the outside, so he wouldn't have to shout or whisper, or perform a striptease. Like a toddler wearing dinner, oblivious, he'd know what he was made of if he were to check the mirror, but why bother. The hardest part was what he'd never see.

FOR A FEW WEEKS THE CLOWN FELL HARD for a Madonna of the Snows, fetching in her perfect cape and shades. It seemed he could never see her eyes, could never read her headlights' dims and brights. She wrapped herself in the delicious velvet-hooded garment of her skin and her subtle exotic plumes, with here and there a stray daub of the pale powder that seemed to follow her and cling, wherever she paused in the petting zoo that passed for her social scene. In this chemical fog with its omnipotent nightly delusions and jagged cement floor wakenings, it took him a few tries to see there was hardly any reaching her, but for feeding her brittle edgy laugh. It snipped around him like shears, making a topiary of his living tree, a sharp bite here and there humbling and redirecting his boisterous self into a flippant green caricature, waving and nodding in her wake.

WHEN PARTYING DRIFTED ONTO the rocks he stopped to wonder what was a party for. Was it merely to share that swirling sense of abandon, that staggering around in the company of other lost souls, that part of them all in lock-step bent on mayhem, on release at any cost? There was the strident brittle noise of booze and drugs, and sure, there came moments for every life in harness, of kicking over traces. Which could make the party a violent dance, a ragged flailing-about that pantomimed rebellion and escape. Yet a holdover hippie residue in him considered a party a utopian ideal, a dance he might join in order to feel joined—good-natured, good-humored, egalitarian. Mating might remain a pressing need, but was never more than part of the dance, nodding and smiling, moving with the others to the beat. A grand or trivial excuse to share company, food and drink—not the raised glass so much as the toasting occasion—reassured that he was welcome, accepted, enjoying a festive give and take, with the ultimate end to share feelings.

CONSIDERING THE STUDENTS HE KNEW, the clown out think-walking noticed how some learners might pass for seat-cushion testers. Yet the fundamental education beginning with Plato and Aristotle involved walking around in dappled shade, in groups who ventured peripatetic musings in the groves of academe. Where the eyes beheld a living changing scene, the mind tried to hew to the discourse, but was endlessly jostled by the body of a world both vast and lightly entertained. So new thoughts flew in and out open windows, perched, made deposits, moved on. While the mind, ever the opportunist, seized on each intrusion as analogy, and proclaimed it as its own.

SO THE MIND PERAMBULATING did work well. Some of it was warming and racing the engine, that blew out cobwebs and carbon. Must be the kind of critters we still are, searching out fresh clues, hunting-gathering. Then without conscious effort the mind on a ramble might sift and reject or improve on whatever it had thought while sitting still. Mentally brought things along for the ride, then sorted to lighten its load. So in our heart of hearts we still must be the kind of wanderers who traveled light as they could, though some packed too heavy to lift, hitched a boxcar to their butterfly for fear of flying.

THE CLOWN HATED THE PHRASE been there, done that. Dismissal born of a checklist, of personal experience that said Don't bother trying to tell me, I already know it all from my one night in a ditch in a blizzard. Some folks seemed to take vacations and see movies and read books only to discuss them in certain knowing ways, to play games of one-upmanship. Some world travelers had this shorthand they'd exchange, evaluating their own and others' experience as a list of exotic places and the deals that got them there, subtle foods they ate, frequent flyer miles racked up, sightings of endangered species, rare celebrities. The recitation seemed to harbor an unspoken question—Are you up to my standards, are you worth being privy to my quantified personal life?

SO TOO HE WEARIED OF HEARING bottom line, and long-story-short. The one was chockfull of financial arrogance, a trump card played as if nothing but money could matter. And the other had no clue what really made a story. Stories were accordions expanded and contracted to sing the moment. The phrase signaled this was one you'd told so often its punchline had worn a groove and needed to be cinched up, right where its belly was dragging.

THEN ONE NIGHT ON THE DOCK the clown drunk met a kindred spirit, sitting drinking in his open fishing boat. Offered him a beer, said he had plenty. Plus he had six brandnew red gas cans full underfoot, and was flicking ashes on them from his cigarette. Threw the butt down in the bilge, lit another. The clown drunk said nothing but the fisherman clown caught his look. Said I just bought em and filled em, want to be the first to know if one leaks. The fisherman clown invited him aboard, but he thought he'd rather sit here dangling his feet, where he might be blown clear.

NEXT MORNING BRIGHT AND EARLY his new friend was out at the end of the dock, cutting open a big cardboard box. He slid out a brand-new Mercury outboard, shiny black, gently laid it on its ear on some newspapers. Then he dumped out eight or ten aerosol paint cans, snatched up a couple and shook them like maracas, till there was a nice even rattling sound. Then still shaking to that rhythm he started spraying the motor. His palette was mosses and khakis, moldy grays, olives, brick reds, dull browns. When he was done the motor looked like it had been fished out of the drink after a year on the bottom. Cheaper than a good lock, he said. You know people. Nobody will touch it for fear they'd catch something.

THE CLOWN WAS COUNTING how many cars passing him had their windows down on this sweltering day. On the freeway it was maybe one in twenty. His ancient car didn't have air-conditioning, but he had the windows down and wore a T-shirt, shorts and sandals, had a squirt bottle to spray on his head, splash down his front and back. He wondered if misery truly loved company. No matter how those bottled up in closed cars stared at him, he didn't feel miserable, just damp, with his clothes sticking to him like that of old folks he had known as a boy. They'd kept cool as they could before somebody conjured this magical bubble, that let them travel all dressed up, not sweating clean through their clothes. But then they'd have missed the aroma of clover and timothy new-mown just now out the window, being turned in the hot sun to cure.

HE WONDERED IF ANYONE EVEN REMEMBERED what people did in the summers before air-conditioning. Rocking or swinging on the porch in the shade. He'd heard old-timers say ladies don't sweat, they glow. And that they used lots of powder. Time was, companies gave out free fans covered with advertising, in churches and courthouses, at funeral homes, county fairs. So folks could conjure a cooling illusion, stir the sultry air round themselves.

HE WAS MOSTLY PAST THE STUPIDITY of drinking, the dependence on it as amusement, medication, distraction or excuse, though never far enough to congratulate himself. It was always there at his elbow in his mind's eye, ready to be sloshed like a sauce on whatever was handy. By then he felt he was stuck as some kind of spokesman for the middle American average white male citizen, when he was anything but. Anti-clown in spite of himself, he didn't like being pegged as the only grownup in the room. He wanted to live in a world of equals, but everywhere he turned seemed set against him, reckless and silly. They'd

93

all say, Come on, man, lighten up, where he craved to respond Heavy down. When he went on jury duty there he was, in his 40s, where everyone else was either just starting out or retired, so by default he was the token grownup. Why not? He paid his taxes, had children in public schools, taught school himself. He seemed to have things sorted out, took an end if a load needed lifting. So they made him foreman, made him sit in the middle and negotiate. Then even deciding a case others old and young got to sit out along the edge and bend the rules.

THE MOMENT CAME AT 46 when his arms shrank, and he needed cheaters. He recalled seeing an old man in a hospital gown and bathrobe spread his newspaper on the floor in a patch of sunlight to read from that great height, and pull his foot out of a slipper to turn the page with his toes. When he came out of the drugstore, he put the glasses on, to see things distant now fuzzy, yet how close his hands were, his scarred knuckles, wrinkles, calluses, the sweep second hand of his wristwatch mowing time now razor-sharp.

THE SKINNY CLOWN KNEW HE NEEDED a fat clown to go with. Preferably also short. The act didn't quite work like a marriage—the choice was for the contrast, the lift and drop. The thing was, how far could you fall off Abbott, before you hit Costello. Likewise Hardy and Laurel. Their quick flips were the essence of jokes, that required a straight man and a zany. Clown mayhem was another matter—Marx Brothers and Stooges all riffing off one another in a maddening round-robin that looked like it had to hurt.

THE HISTORY TEACHER CLOWN was remembering Ike—farm-boy Dwight D. Eisenhower, whose name meant hewer of iron. How when the war broke out he was still a colonel. But the old guys needed a new guy to take orders from, so Marshall picked and promoted him. McArthur that preening prima donna couldn't help posturing, shooting his mouth off, making it all about himself. Montgomery would have faltered and shoveled blame around, while Patton would have got to the outskirts of Moscow without a drop left in the tank, throwing rocks at the Russkies. None of the rabid dogs of war would have held up to the demands of this shitstorm wider than any of them dreamt. They needed to be leashed and muzzled by a diplomat clown who could keep his mouth shut, who appeared to bumble but hardly ever did.

HE FIRST READ ALBERT SCHWEITZER'S The Quest of the Historical Jesus in high school, in secret, and said not one word about it. Inoculated by past experience, he didn't check to see if it was on the Index, didn't want to know if such a sensible humanitarian could occasion mortal sin. The Jesuits taught him faith and obedience, and made clever use of reason and rhetoric to nail down everything else. But suddenly here was a new thought, whether, how and where an actual Jesus lived— and what historians might make of available evidence. Over the next ten years he got deeper into textual scholarship, chewed through a few medieval scriptural exegeses, studied a little ancient politics, and learned a whole new set of reasons to distrust any literal interpretation of a document he couldn't read in the original. Not to mention laboring through Josephus, Bishop Irenaeus, the Gnostic Gospels and the Council of Nicaea in 325, setting up a state religion that would make Pontius Pilate out to be a sweetheart, and blame the death of the Christ on the Jews.

THERE WAS PROFICIENCY, then there was learning dressed as mayhem, as serious fun. At the school where he taught, a young clown was practicing falling down stairs. The stairs were carpeted, had a landing halfway that took a turn to the left, so it was vital to keep up one's momentum, negotiate the obstacle without stalling midway. This one clown was getting good at it, made a clatter like a broken-down carnival ride, that drew the clown teacher nearby to come see what was up. Suddenly eyes were averted, lips sealed. So he said Show me. And got to watch the clown setup at the top, the oblivious saunter and misstep, the exaggerated whoopsie, the frightened double-take, the tuck and roll, the rubber body flail clean to the bottom. The rumpled heap there held a beat, that drew a burst of applause. The clown teacher commended his technique, his unbridled magnificence, quoted the immortal Buster Keaton on how to take a fall, then made them swear off forever.

ON THE WAY SAILING WITH HIS SON the clown stopped to call his father, towing the boat on a trailer coast to coast. He invited him to come along, said there were three bunks, but the old man growled No way. It was the same call he'd made from Ketchikan several years before. Then eight weeks later on the way home they stopped in Ohio to visit him for a few days. The place was fancy, wouldn't let them park the trailered boat there, so they found a storage lot a mile or two away. Then when the visit was done, they said their goodbyes at the entrance to the fancy place, and headed to the lot to hook up their boat trailer. When they got inside the fence, there was the old man outside, fingers laced through the chainlink, quietly watching all they did. He had gotten in his car and followed them. The second goodbye was harder than the first, handshakes and embraces more final, already emptied of words.

DRIVING EAST TO VISIT HIS AILING FATHER 2900 miles off, he needed a tooth fixed first. It was a large tricky filling, that he didn't want to let go on the road, so asked how long till it could stand to be chewed on. The dentist said it would be at 80% strength in 12 hours. With his mouth numb as stovewood he mumbled When would it be 100? The dentist said maybe 20 hours, but clearly thought the question silly. Just baby it, he said. So, loaded and gassed, he headed for the freeway, with his stomach already grumbling. But he was not about to take a bite that could bite him back. Then on the far side of night, with the sky paling to the east, the 20 hours was up. He pulled into a truck stop in Sublett, Idaho. When he got to the counter he could already smell something his mother used to make, vegetable soup with beef bones, bay leaves, plenty of onions and garlic, carrots, potatoes, leftover green beans and whatnot. Behind the counter was a handsome woman with a little gray in her hair, with an easy, lovely way about her. Ignoring the menu he asked her to bring him some of what smelled so good. He ate four bowls without biting down on anything. And by the time he was full he considered proposing on his knees to this woman who could cook the old magic, though when he tried to talk through his sore mug she only laughed and turned away.

WHEN THE CLOWN CAME TO VISIT his father these days he stayed till the old man was sick of him, then got over it. That was how love worked. So he wouldn't feel so bad when his son had to travel the thousands of miles back to work, and would be gone so long again. There were these chasms between them, these unpardonable differences, but there was also this bond. The old man would drink and go on the attack, and for years drew blood any way he could. Shouting I made love for you! But by now he was down to saying You know you've wasted your life, you could have done anything, you could have gone to the top. The clown would savor the tired delusions, the impossibilities, laugh and say If you say so. That was enough, plenty, because the old man had heard his side of it all before, and neither of them needed to mount a full-scale grand opera. Maybe cross wooden swords, skirmish a bit for honor's sake, but not fight the last war all over.

THE CLOWN'S FATHER HATED FALL, sulked while the piles of dead leaves crackled underfoot, set to molder in the damp days darkening. Of course some of that was the chuckhole of his birthday, past full barns and harvest moons, that always threatened an axle. There was no talking him out of it, his forlorn cheerlessness had been thrown down the well to make everything taste of it. He also refused to eat cake, though he would blow out a candle stuck in a good slice of pie.

FOR HIS FATHER'S 70th BIRTHDAY, so far away and deep into the teaching season, the clown went to a costume shop and bought the whole bin of clown noses—three dozen in all. Then he wrote a note that said Some party favors to lighten the moment. Pass them around. I hope you all have a grand time. The red plastic honkers arrived days before the party, but nobody ever mentioned seeing one. After the old man died he half-expected to find that bag of noses among his effects. But they must have landed wrong, and got pitched in a fit of anger.

UNLIKE HIS DAD IN FALL the clown didn't bother hating anything astir in the natural world. It was mostly beautiful, even skidding on wet leaves, even overwhelming hits that reduced you to jelly, made you hunker down or run, a hailstone white-out, mudslide or windstorm or lightning. He looked forward to the mud, then snow, then ice, then more mud, naked wet black branches, changes on and on, and through it all the string of footprints that followed wherever he wandered, the lovely feel of a fire on a bitter night reaching down through skin and muscle clothing the chilly body deep into his bones.

THE CLOWN'S DAD NEVER HAD A DOG when he was young. His dad's dad had a mean dog Jack, an ugly slobbering thing chained to a hundred-foot steel cable outside the hen house in the Depression, to run off weasels, foxes, hungry drifters, to guard their chicken business. From age twelve to sixteen his dad had to sleep with the chickens, tend his dad's investment, kill and pluck 300 every Saturday. The old man worked the night shift on the railroad, slept the days out, and had a phone line strung out to the hen house so he could wake his son every few hours for a poultry report, to turn on the heater if the temperature dropped, keep them not too cool or too hot, keep feed and water coming. When the bank foreclosed on the little farm in '33, his dad said he secretly hoped he might get to be a kid again, but never did.

THEY FINALLY TALKED ABOUT THE WAR. When the worst-of-all-time for his father came after battles, on the hospital ship stuffed with the wounded and dying. Every bed taken, men dying on cots in the passageways, on deck under tarps rigged for shade. When the CO and his second-in-command would make themselves scarce, pour themselves drinks in their cabins, leave it to novice doctors to patch the bloody horrors off the beach that just kept coming. Then exhausted dazed times would arrive when the days ran together, when no one in the OR knew any more than he did, when he would have to stabilize the patient, retreat to his bunk, dig out textbooks and notebooks, beyond words and pictures improvise what would have to be done.

THE CLOWN'S SICK DAD TOLD HIM about his own dad's final days in the hospital, neglected when he got officious and evil-tempered, which, no surprise, was right when the nurses got scarce. The old railroad yardmaster with a 4th grade education had had to go on a bedpan, couldn't move so good, and shit himself. Just then his son's boss and friend came by to say hello and check on him. And this eminent neurosurgeon shook his shit-covered hand, insisted on it, then found some towels to clean them both off and share a laugh at their precious dignity.

FOR EIGHT YEARS AFTER HE RETIRED at 70, the old doctor like a small boat in heavy seas rode the painful surges of the body up and down. At first he was ready to give it up, starve himself along with the cancers, keep up the drinking and smoking, expecting his anger and despair to pop a gasket and finish him. But then he accepted the ride, saw that there might at least be some moments worth living for. That with all these kids and their kids, even dying he could show how it might be done. So on he went through bowel cancer, lung cancer, a broken hip, colostomy bags and a bowel resection, then metastasis, and lesions on the brain. The ride harder since he could see it all coming, knew precisely what was in store. There could be no horseplay about his prognosis, no avoiding thoughts of the disheartening loss of function, the body's failures that could erode any pride in accomplishment, drown all sense of self in a rising tide of pain.

WHEN HIS FATHER WAS DYING he gave up drinking and smoking, that for years had lingered around his sick bed—bad-boy acts of defiance all he had left to mock the implacable powers-that-be. Or were these just holdovers from the war? Now he said They don't do a thing for me anymore. Said They must have cut that part out of me. Still he'd ask for a drink at cocktail hour, and have a cigarette lit, just in case the craving doubled back. Said he liked the look of it there. But for that last couple months he let the ice melt and sweat on the coaster, the lit cigarette burn down to the filter untouched. They reminded the clown of offerings at gravesides laid out fresh, deliberately left to molder.

THE OLD MAN WANTED HIM THERE when he died. He never said why, and the clown never asked. After the eight-year parade of illnesses, they had an understanding. He wanted it private, he wanted no arguments over what was to happen and why, he wanted the clown there—but for what? To hold onto maybe. Bear witness and share. If he wanted to die at home in his own bed, even for a doctor everything had to be just so, all the possible questions answered in advance. This was his escape. Otherwise they'd bundle him back to the hospital in an aid car blazing and wailing, hook him up to machines, pump back in a little painful useless momentary life, and make him do it all over, climb that rocky hill, look out again and let go, gasp another final breath.

AND NOW WHAT, BESIDES LIVING for oneself? With his father gone he had his naked self to reconsider—whether living stacked up any better than firewood, and what that meant. He was quiet but not broken, though for a year or two he kept off to himself. He had taken early retirement from teaching, that had relied on chin music, the sharpened attention and clacking jawbone he now was reluctant to work. So he took up the slighter melodies of printing in the shop. There was the faint clickety-click of letters dropped into the type stick, then the creaking treadle that drove the press through its jingle, ratchet and clank, the rollers passed over the ink disk and type lockup with a sound like tearing silk, then the clunk as it all came together, that definite lingering kiss, then the yawn and release.

SADNESS WAS NOT TRAGEDY, nor a slack excuse for mopery. Past a certain point life was loss, the train pulling out irregardless, with no spare tissues to blow, no embroidered hankies. A fall from a height due to a character flaw was tragic, unless the height was a stepladder balanced on the cleft chin of your fully garbed clown by the bald light of day, that couldn't be mounted or clumb.

HIS CHILDREN EASED ON INTO ADULTHOOD like it was a ghost town off the freeway, both unpredictably frivolous and deeply serious. Were clowns fashioned out of such seesaw materials? Things could be worse. They already knew how to search and find joy for themselves, in themselves, and what that felt like, not just in others passing through their swinging doors. Best of all they knew how to open the hand, share in the moment what mattered, ripe and whole.

NOT ALL MIDDLE-AGED CLOWNS WERE SET to be grandparents, though he was. Nothing competes with a baby clown's laughter or tears. But the choice was not his but his kids'. And what did they want? A whole different world, cooler and calmer, with fewer people, fewer cars, fewer wars. Maybe more lovers hand in hand strolling sidewalks, more jugglers, dreamers and tumblers in the open air. Fewer corporate profiteers who built nothing, made nothing, bankrupted and preyed on the rest of us. Not so many malls, more little mom and pop stores. Slower food with less catsup, more flavor, colder and tastier beer. He saw how their lack of children amounted to an indictment: fix things or else it grinds to a halt here. The trouble was, it seemed only baby clowns had the power to yank parents out of the rut of the past, and conjure a sweet far-off future.

WHEN HE WAS 56 THE CLOWN AT LAST taught himself how to juggle. He got some jaunty beanbags and practiced an hour a day by the clock standing over his bed, where he didn't have so far to bend when they dropped. And drop they did. For eight days he tossed up the beanbags, one-two-three-drop, one-two-three-drop, the fourth always eluding his fingertips as he reached for it. He tried different ways of holding and tossing, snuck in extra practice time, but then late in the hour of the eighth day, he caught it. And by the ninth day he could juggle practically nonstop, bouncing them off the ceiling, staggering around the room, ecstatic. He had wanted to juggle and had tried to learn since he was fifteen but couldn't do it back when he was nimble and the world was young. Why not? His fifty-six-year-old self answered that he couldn't take that much failure, with no touch or taste of success. But if that was so, what about this endless writing stuff? He knew that for every piece that shone there were dozens of also-rans, and dozens more that outright flopped. And hundreds composted beyond that. And in all that dream rubble, a few tosses so high in the air they might still be caught.

THE CLOWN GOT WORD HIS FAVORITE maiden aunt was ailing, in the hospital. He went to a florist and arranged to have her favorite made up and sent to her, a little cactus garden in a shallow pot, half a dozen varieties with several already blooming, yellow, red and white. He wrote and signed the card, then went home and arranged to call her a couple days later, when the cacti would have arrived, when she'd be awake near a phone. When he called she was glad to hear from him, said he sounded the same as always, and after a while she told him she'd just gotten a wonderful gift—from his parents. She explained how this long-dead couple were in Arizona vacationing, and had sent her a miniature garden. So thoughtful, she said, savoring a long-gone but still potent moment from forty years before, when he'd been a child. Tiptoeing so as not to break the spell, he leaned close to hear her softly explain how she had the perfect spot to plant these hardy little lives, by the kitchen door, right where they'd been growing forever.

workaday whirl

"A hungry clown is half mad." –French proverb

ONE THING ABOUT FARMING HE LOVED, you didn't have to go to work, you lived at work, no matter what else you did it was there in the open all round. Like cows watching you hang wet laundry on the line. The hard part was fitting your distracted self into your days on the ground. Especially with breakdowns, repairs. Like the pickup with its hood off, the starter set out for its final ride into town. Sure, you could give it too much or too little, and farmers said there was no money, but between plants and animals, old folks and kids, migrating birds and butterflies, long days then long rest, there was more than enough of a living.

WORKING ON CARS HE LEARNED some deceptions require the whole banana. One mechanic he knew who worked for a used-car dealer, selling a car with a howling rear-end, would shove a whole green banana, skin and all, into the filler hole. He said that would quiet the worn gears for about eighty miles, just enough to get the car off the lot and away to a new home before the howling returned with a vengeance. This Banana Rebuild was better than sawdust, about like duct tape repairs that held the floppy sole to your shoe till you were off and running.

AND HE'D HEARD OLD FARMERS TELL about what they called a Duco Rebuild, where grease and dirt would be cleaned off the outside of old equipment, which would then be spraypainted in fresh factory colors. He briefly worked for a boss who painted a Triumph TR-3 engine after he'd given it a tuneup and oil change, said You made it run so fine it oughta been a rebuild — a sign that that job wouldn't last.

TO MAKE SOME CHRISTMAS MONEY the young clown and his brother rebuilt an engine in an MG roadster. The garage where they worked had an improvised heater like troops used in Korea, with a big tank full of gasoline high on the far wall, a copper fuel line with a valve that ran downhill into the steel oil drum sitting on concrete blocks, with a flue pipe that ran out the top through the roof, and a door on hinges welded to one side. To work it you opened the petcock a little, got the gas dripping into the barrel, then tossed in a match. Pretty soon the barrel would be glowing red down one side, and you'd need to turn it down. Everybody knew it might blow, and after a while hearing it roar felt a little like getting shot at. But your choices were like the army's—freeze or make jokes or shut up.

USED TO BE WITH BENCH SEATS and no seatbelts any car could be a clown car. Just paper over the windows, leave a thin slit to see through. For more seating you took out the seats and sat on each other. Then all it took was practice getting in and out, a method to your madness. When you wanted to lurch pop the clutch. To make it backfire turn the key off and on once you're rolling.

IT STRUCK THE CLOWN MECHANIC how cars were like people, with that crazy mix of mechanics, plumbing and wiring, all those fluids and impulses to check and time and keep separate. No engineer would have designed a human like this. But from the dawn of the industrial age, machines were built to imitate humans, complete with stagger-starts and reciprocal motions, alternations and imbalances, huffing and moaning and farting. The thing was, you could make a steam-powered baby that needed constant care, but then couldn't give it a steam-powered brain to watch the tracks ahead or feed itself. So cars kept mocking those risky improbable humans with their mix of dumbs and smarts, tried to calm conflicting impulses and keep their juices straight. But so what—airplanes still couldn't flap their wings on take-off.

ONE NIGHT HE SET PINS in an old bowling alley, trying out for a job in a place that couldn't afford the fancy new Brunswick machines. He'd only bowled a couple times, and this was like being part janitor part jockey, perched up above his lane where he would clean up the mess, stuff pins in the rack and reset them. It was like playing bingo, chaotic yet a place for everything, getting pins to drop on their spots with no waste motion. Even tucked out of the way, invisible, he could sense out front the bowlers taking turns, nervous patter full of bravado, flirtation, street psychology, the drama of the skidding launch and roll down the alley that might drift off a gutterball or hook a strike that practically jumped up and bit him. But after an hour or two the novelty wore thin, the crashing made his ears ring, and he called it quits.

HE SPOKE DIRECTLY AND POLITELY to waiters and guards, cashiers and window clerks, because just often enough his knock at the stranger's door had been answered. Right when they were needed, his mail carrier or UPS driver had proven a person of inspiration and insight, of secret but sterling accomplishments. Besides, he'd been a clerk and salesman and mechanic every bit as anonymous. Another red door down a block of red doors, shut to every passerby till a friendly knock, where it took one to know one, as a fellow worker opened up.

WORKING AS A CLERK-TYPIST he learned the hard way that people didn't want their spelling and grammar corrected. Not really. And it didn't much matter—you could mostly tell what they meant. So cleaning up mistakes was a thankless nuisance, the display of a finicky showoff. A sign of education that by half the population was undervalued and dismissed. Businesses let him know they could hire a clown like him for pennies to clean up their act. Too bad folks in casinos didn't play Scrabble for cash.

IN THIS SUMMER JOB HE GOT TRAPPED in a sewer sludge of paperwork. Hospital bills in quintuplicate to be sorted, collated, distributed. From in-box to out-box, no way to go any faster, do more, feel any sense of accomplishment. So he started writing a novel on letterhead stationery. Each page would start with an address to someone in a department of this vast enterprise, in case someone peeked over his shoulder, then carry on with the story. So he could rattle away at breakneck speed, ostensibly doing what everyone hated.

THE SUMMER BEFORE HE WENT WEST he hooked up with a temp agency that had no call for MAs in English—but he was persuasive, versatile, desperate. Since they had the lock on the job, he got paid half for his work, while the agency kept the other half. His best and hardest job was as mailboy for a large corporation's home office. They paid him to shadow the mailboy around for a week, then do the guy's job for two weeks while he was on vacation. Before computers, the mail both internal and external was voluminous and Byzantine. With 400 offices and cubicles he had to learn the pecking order, the secret structure that included both what the eighty vice-presidents' titles meant and what they actually did, how the power slid down the slushy mountain over these hot summer days. So he took and used copious notes. At the end the president's executive secretary who really ran the place said he was the best she had seen, and asked if he'd like a real job. She had the grace to be embarrassed when he told her how much schooling he had. Their mailboy was the son of a company higher-up, a forty-year-old high school dropout who had had the job since his teens. He had invented the convoluted and obscure methods they were afraid to tamper with, that had to be learned by someone anew every summer, so he could go off and play.

THAT FIRST DAWN STEPPING INTO a classroom felt like coming home. It was the bottom rung, an anonymous slot on a campus swarming with 36,000 students, at 7:30 am heading into the tunnel of fall, that he came to without training except for his own student agonies, and grading papers for professors the previous four years. He suddenly saw as he stood before this sleepy crew how much he had craved this chance, how many tricks he had tucked in his bag, how many notions he was set to try. For teachers there were no easy measures of success, and these were troubled times, so jobs came and went, but lobbying and diplomacy never occurred to him, being foreign to the venture. He knew this was a firing-line job, not entertainment, and such jobs came to those who could do them, and under duress could keep doing them. Though many colleagues would fall in the trenches, and a few would advance, he never looked for a battlefield promotion, since there was no harder or more worthy work on earth.

THE CLOWN'S SUMMER JOB WAS DRIVING a six-ton delivery truck, running around loading and unloading bundles of cardboard boxes all day long. He got a nickel more than minimum wage, which was soon raised to a dime since he went at it so hard, had the moves, didn't let moss grow anywhere he rolled. At that he was still broke and desperate, glad to be working at all, trying to figure what to do with the schooling he had, since teaching jobs had dried up. At home there was a pile of books to be read, and a pile of his scribbles, but the job started in the alley behind J.C. Penny's at 6 am sharp, with the winos already calling, Hey Red, you wanna go in on a bottle?

LATE IN THE DAY DELIVERING bundles of boxes to a mattress & pillow factory along Interbay, he parked the truck and lugged the first bundle in. He couldn't see across the floor of the huge wooden room, where a blizzard of goose down hung on the still air. He looked around through drifts and swirls of tiny feathers, saw long wooden tables where women and girls stuffed pillows, cushions and comforters, and sewed them shut by hand. No one wore a paper mask. Their brown faces glowed in the heat, and feathers clung like the snow of age to their dark hair, to their damp arms and hands. This was truly a sweat shop—no open windows, no fans. Huffing the boxes in he felt embarrassed for them, shamed and powerless. Yet the powdered heads upturned to watch him conjured angels— flashed through the mounting gloom of that cavern their dazzling smiles.

HE FOUND THE BEST WORK BOOTS at Goodwill, high-top rough rawhide with bits of walnut shell cast into red rubber soles and heels, like some car tires they used to make. The boots were a perfect fit, the kind nobody would ever think to shine, and had great traction, but took forever to take off and put on, since there were no hooks for the leather laces, only eyes. Eventually it dawned on him these were convict shoes, from some chain-gang prison farm where the wearer had all the time in the world to get dressed and undressed, while some guard yelled Hurry up.

THE TRUCKER JOB ATE a pair of leather gloves a week. Loading and unloading truckloads of corrugated cardboard he went though pair after pair, ambidextrous wore out both hands evenly, and if he tried to stretch another week came home with bloody fingers, which made it hard to play guitar. So on the calendar he counted out the weeks to go, and shopped around for a deal.

THEN CAME A COUPLE YEARS OF DRIVING city bus, where he learned to see roads as rivers, where the current flowed stronger in some lanes than others. There was always a best lane to be in. Trouble was, every route was made up of stops. So he was forced to dip into and out of eddies, backwaters, blocked and cut off by cars and trucks, competing with everything out there for right of way, even sleepy pedestrians and wayward invisible bikes. So he kept his window wide and worked his left-hand gestures—pleading for an opening, counseling patience, pointing out where he needed to go, waving thanks to whoever let him in. Signaling questions, warnings, joking thumbs up and thumbs down, stop and go, snake moves and chopper moves.

ONE FOGGY MORNING AT 4:18 heading out to the end of the line for the first run into town, the bus driver clown got stuck in traffic, waiting for a parade up 4th Avenue from the south end rail-yard clear to the Space Needle. An elephant procession led the way, trunks holding each others' tails, followed by zebras and camels and ponies clattering along, sleepy and obedient. Then came cages on wheels pulled by horses, while inside lions and tigers paced and roared. Then gaudy trucks and gilded caravans, and at last a professor clown in full makeup wearing top hat and gloves playing a horse-drawn steam calliope, who sent circus tunes rattling down the dark empty canyons, announcing who had arrived and would shortly be open for business two shows a day.

THE BUS DRIVER CLOWN HIT THE BRAKES hard at the end of South Park Bridge, stopped within inches of the little boy on his tricycle who had toppled off the high sidewalk into his path. He hit the flashers, sprang from the seat and set the three-year-old and his buggy back up next to his mother, who had her hands full wheeling a cart full of groceries. He didn't wait to watch while she snatched up the little one. He was running late, should already be turned around heading out, but had a dozen riders in this neighborhood still to get home, maybe a few shaken up. Though as they pulled the cord and got off it seemed as if no one had seen or felt a thing. So no need to bother with an Incident Report that would make him late for supper, and squeezing his own little ones.

THE BUS DRIVER CLOWN HAD a black bus driver friend who admired his sunglasses that were way too dark. He'd bought them down in the Southwest desert one day so bright it hurt his eyes. Now in the rainy Northwest he was apt to miss an old person or kid lurking in the shadows unless he peeled the glasses back for a better look. So one bright day he gave them to his friend who looked great in them and had no trouble spotting passengers. He even wore them to his house for a party, danced up a storm, never once took them off, never bumped into a thing.

HE PICKED UP A BLIND MAN for the morning rush into town, running late, unshaven, flailing his cane and briefcase, his tie a red noose round his neck. He let the man off on Second Avenue with the rest of the load, then looped around the block to head back north. But then at a stoplight he looked into an empty tavern and there sat the man in a splash of summer sun, with a first drink in front of him, cinching up his tie, putting himself together at quarter to eight in the morning. He thought everyone must have such naked moments, when all they could do was sit still and pray to be overlooked.

BUS DRIVING HE HAD A SHOWDOWN with the obvious. He was a writer, yet nothing in print paid the rent or fed the kids. Art was free as yesterday's newspaper. And as far as the world was concerned he was no artist, he was part of a system that chauffeured those who couldn't get a car or driver's license, which made him marginally useful, a mild necessity to the powers that be. After all, poor folks had to get to work and the store, somehow cast their puny economic vote. He let one guy haul a ten-foot Christmas tree onto the bus in the middle of one drizzly day. Risked getting caught and written up, although not by a writer. Luckily no boss was looking. He had all that room, and how else would the guy get it home?

THE BUS DRIVER CLOWN FELT IRRELEVANT. Just a nut at the wheel over-torqued. Most days he did the job perfectly, though it was tough to follow not just intricate routes but endless rules. The eighty-year-old system that had seen and done everything worked nonstop to trim his ego, show him how this world was designed to function, made clear he was not the boss of anything, not one little bit. That it was silly to call it his bus even sitting in the seat with the engine running. If they'd left him a place to stand, allowed him more than a splash and a hint, he might have stayed till they hauled him off to the bone yard. As it was after two years, threadbare and expendable, forced to accept his uniformed self as part of the equipment, he quit.

IN HIS PRIMAL BUS-DRIVER NIGHTMARE it was always night and raining, and the clown would be driving an electric trolley that had gone off its overhead, lost its poles. So he'd have to turn on the flashers, pull down on the ropes, get each shoe in position, and be looking up wet-faced when there'd be a blinding blue-white-purple flash as it touched the wire. And there he'd be, blinking like an owl in a blast furnace, and couldn't see to set the other shoe.

THE BUS-DRIVER NIGHTMARE FOR HIM was a version of the actor's nightmare—where am I supposed to be, what do I do and say, who am I. He'd be late and in a hurry to get to a relief point where the bus just sat there running. He'd have lost his punch and transfers and run card, so he'd have to get out in the street in the rain and look up at the big lit signboard, to get a clue. Or he'd have to wake up a sleepy passenger and ask which bus this was, where it went. Or flag down another bus at an intersection and throw himself at the mercy of some old timer, beg for transfers and a schedule, maybe borrow his punch for a minute, while the old guy scowled and shook his head at the clown's ineptitude. Though he'd had a few minutes of panic, as a waking operator he had never been this slack. Actually he had a perfect record, never an accident, hardly even a minor complaint, so for thirty years afterward bus driving was his fallback. If all else fell through, with his record he knew he'd be hired in a minute, and get tossed back into the huge crazy system that had always been sink or swim. Which must be why the dreams kept bubbling up.

BUT THE NIGHTMARES WERE MADE OF real stuff, more's the pity. The old woman who shouted at the clown, demanding he stop in the middle of the block at her house, because she was carrying groceries. The poor bastard of a trolley bus driver in the middle of the night who'd lost his poles and rolled out from under the overhead, who begged him to push his bus back under so he wouldn't have to call for a wrecker and get written up. The woman in rush hour who climbed aboard with a gallon of soy sauce and ten pounds of rice cradled in her arms like two babies, both of which she dropped and split open, to decorate the ankles and shoes of a standing load of passengers. And the parade of teenagers who would give him transfers days old and complain when he finally caught one out of a dozen and made him pay. Some days he would have traded the pope washing the feet of the poor, or Solomon chopping babies.

HIS LATEST BUS DRIVER DREAM wasn't much of a nightmare. For the first time the old clown seemed to be some kind of boss, an Inspector instead of what they called an Operator. He was surveying a line with an old boss he had worked for, teaching English. No telling why this guy was along for the ride, keeping mum. Suddenly they came upon a bus dead at a stop. It was an odd vehicle, very tall, with the driver sitting out front and overhead, like a crane operator. The driver was a serious young woman. He leaned way back to talk to her about what had gone wrong. She said she'd pulled into this stop for a layover, shut it down for a few minutes, then couldn't get it to turn over. He said Come on down, let me try. Right away he knew what it was, the starter bendix stuck in the flywheel teeth, that had happened to him, cost him an hour waiting for a wrecker with the flashers on, parked in traffic. So he got everyone out of the bus to push on either end, rock it back and forth till the starter popped loose and he woke up happy as a clam.

ON THE LAST DAY OF A DREAM JOB as the city's Playwright-in-Residence, the clown was returning books to the University Library, crossing a sunlit parking lot when two campus cops stopped him, demanded he show them ID. They were younger than he was, looked seriously fit. He sat down his bag on the blacktop, asked what this was about. The cop in front of him unsnapped his gun and put his hand on it, while the other got on a radio. The first said Just show us ID. So he did. The one with his hand on his gun said State your business. He told them he was an artist, had this job that let him check out University books. That were due today. They looked back and forth from him to his driver's license, then the second one poked through his books, mostly medieval Muslim history. While they were at it he said he had taught here four years, and the cops never carried guns then. The one with his hand on his gun said Times change.

HE GOT A JOB WORKING WITH minority teenagers in the inner city, who were living in group homes. These were clean safe places, but the kids were always squabbling, on the verge of trouble, always running away. When one boy went back to juvenile detention for stealing and wrecking a car, the staff found some stolen stuff under his bed, that the clown tried hard to give back. There was a box of colored slides, some family's complete history, a record of smiling sober faces at vacations, weddings, birthdays, graduations, anniversaries, funerals. He loaded the faded slides into a projector and watched them over and over for clues. But it was way too personal. Why bother to steal and hide someone else's history? The other thing was a memento of catastrophe, a big silver pocket watch that had been through a fire. Its blackened face was left telling the one thing it knew, the moment fire shattered the crystal and bubbled the silver.

THE CLOWN FEELING SOMETIMES ARRIVED when he turned on the job he was paid for, told himself there was no such thing as a bad job, then instantly spun on his heel and saw if that was true, there was also no such thing as a good job, if by job you meant something done strictly for pay. So was there no good or bad paycheck? Did all work have an extrinsic value, worth only what others were willing to pay on the open market? And what if the market was rigged, what if there were bosses and companies never satisfied till they paid nothing, who plotted the return of slavery? What if he loved what he did, couldn't quit doing it no matter what? What if he owned what he did so deeply he couldn't part with it, could only share, loan it out for a while, pass it on to the next caretaker?

SO FOR A WHILE HE BECAME ADEPT at burning bridges, even the kind made of sterner less flammable stuff. As each job ended he had an overwhelming urge to tell the old boss what had been going on, what he really felt. Face to face or in a detailed letter set things straight. He could be diplomatic, but some things needed nailing down. The one hitch came if he needed a reference. But he'd had several jobs that might qualify as torture, where more was demanded and endured than money could begin to compensate. But then along the way he also woke to the fact that all bosses wanted more for less, that's just how they were wired, so the first duty of an employee was to contain expectations, draw boundaries—like a boxer go into a crouch, protect himself.

AS A TEACHER HE QUICKLY SAW how little age mattered—but how much time did. Once kids suspected they'd need to understand not just specialized parts of the puzzle, but how it all fit together, they should be wanting to learn all the time, as much and as fast as they could. Learning stuff for which no one mind could ever be smart enough, or move quick enough. Study that made your brain swell like bread dough. The truth was, the whole of us needed to know everything. So his job was to waken students, be unpredictable, playful while serious. Ask hard questions. Joke away despair. Help them figure things out not just for themselves but for each other. Insist they own their answers. See how they fit into groups, worked together. He'd studied developmental psychology, but also sensed that the little person looking out of her crib was the same one who would be looking out of her marriage bed, peering up from her work bench, watching sunset from her death bed. Memories wound like vines on an armature of the self. What we were each working on might constitute an identity, but in groups there was more at stake. In leaps we might learn who we were becoming as a species, as social creatures who might smarten each other and share the good stuff, not fight to the death over it.

PLUS HE HAD THS HAREBRAINED THEORY that the exceptional teacher might have to be coaxed, even tricked out of his innermost secrets, since those secrets might have cost his life, so might be death to broadcast. It was part of the job of the student to convince the teacher that he might catch on quickly, at least eventually, and would do work worthy of the master's investment and trust. The mysteries of a craft were elusive, might have been stumbled on or dawned only after years of diligence, so the master might be incapable of surrendering his insights, without sensing a promise not to be squandered or lost.

HE WAS HAVING TROUBLE WITH COFFEE, just as the fancy brew business took off. Because he couldn't sip just a little, went at it all day, worked where they just kept making a fresh pot, then fought the jitters on into the night. It got like a junkie story, the scoured bowels, gut like a starving caged bobcat. Nothing worse than not sleeping where you finally made the dog lie down right around time to get up. So he quit coffee, and had this ice pick stuck out his left frontal lobe for three days. That metal handle zinged him, caught every chilly little breeze. Then he switched to tea and held hard at two cups, slept more, still managed somehow to wake up.

TEACHING KIDS THE SAME AGES AS HIS OWN was a secret gift to the clown parent. He could see how much of their shared dance was age-inappropriate, a kind of group foray to be shepherded and suffered through as they gesticulated wildly back and forth. But then some of their antics showed the footwork of unique demons, hinted at the kind of grownups they'd become. Provided they got dance lessons, and a little encouragement.

THEY SAY YOU CAN CHOOSE to greet the day with hope or attitude. Then there were those who took an upper and a downer and let 'em fight it out. But the teacher clown met a girl who'd announce to one and all I'm in a bad mood, like that was fair warning, and a day-long pass. Maybe it was her way to signal her monthly curse, that no one would look forward to, unless they'd been involved in some risky playtime and lost count. And yes, she was cute, but nowhere near cute enough for how down and ugly things might get. Some days clowning was all that got you through without hard feelings. But some who knew it took two to tangle still honked their horn and yelled Look out, here, I'm coming through!

SOME CLOWNS ASKED QUESTIONS to find answers, and some to find more questions. Knowing how mysteries outdistance us, how as we shine light in the cave undiscovered nothings scurry off. How some ideas once caught chew themselves free, roam at large forgotten, only ages later recaught. Like why fish don't sleep. Like the wolverine's mating dance. Like humans forgetting how to swim since that dark night we crawled ashore. If firewalkers' feet are ticklish. How birds go from baby to adult in that one step out of the nest. How lightning chooses where to strike. Why some trees have a corkscrew grain where their siblings are perfectly straight. Why kneesocks hardly ever touch your knees. What the ivory billed woodpecker hammers to her mate. How the ginkgo decides when to drop its leaves. If honeybees can get lost. How the IRS picks you for an audit.

WHAT THE OLD FOLKS NEVER SAID about work was how soon you lost energy and focus, how life conspired to eat your lunch along with your sleep and best efforts. So you made these trade-offs, learned to take naps, party less. The boss was always looking to replace you with someone younger and dumber, with more energy to burn, who'd work for minimum wage. On the flip side, nobody wanted a job just to show what they could have done if they'd had to. Even if the sole reason to take the job was money, there was still no excuse for doing nothing, running out the clock in a make-believe pretense of busy-ness, polishing the fire truck.

SUDDENLY WITHOUT STUDENTS, the clown dug into the ancient craft of letterpress printing. Handset handbound books with lead type and actual woodcuts. Approached by others wanting to learn from him he savored the eastern notion that the student might sweep out the shop and make tea, do little but do it perfectly. Yet he watched the thought dawn on an erstwhile apprentice that humility could never be enough, that time's march was relentless, that if the master could squander his time he might as well skip the mocking laughs and stern looks and go squander it himself. Then too he saw how many looking to be students these days had their own agendas, didn't want to learn to do by doing, just wanted to play with the toys and speak knowingly of the craft. They somehow missed the point that every astronaut was a scientist first and last, a pilot and technician, not a glorified tourist bumped up to first class.

AFTER ALL THE STUDY AND PLANNING just to make a start, life amounted to a feeling in the body, where some doings soon felt like a misfit, maybe a waste, maybe self-destructive, maybe too much abstraction or too much thoughtless effort, not what mattered enough to keep him coming back to it every morning. And it wasn't mostly the money. Some doings just felt right. Over time such feelings might change, so he might have to change with them, or become a sad clown, a helpless captive in his life. There was magic in one's drive to be located and nourished, even if he never told another soul about it, even if he had no words for the telling. Everything else was marking time till he learned by doing what that was, what drew and held him, what stoked his engine till it chuffed and whistled.

THERE WAS THAT OLD SAYING it takes one to know one. But were clowns not also cops, crooks, truckers, waiters, ex-lover hedge fund tweakers, ex-jock ex-presidents, performers looking to turn pro, back-stage cultured pearls for the nonce short-order cooks? Whoever worked could use a kind word, a free cookie. The shock of recognition might hit even passing through crowds of strangers while glued to your latest app. And the working self was a construct, fragile or resilient, concocted of what was on hand however unlikely, a silly flag of convenience, a patchwork sail of bar napkins set to the prevailing breeze, lowered out of despair or raised in hope as need be.

the mysteries

"There are truths that are singularly shy and ticklish and cannot be caught except suddenly—truths that must be surprised or left alone."
                                      –Nietzsche, The Gay Science

THERE WAS THE ALLURE OF looking up and out into the sky, fleeing his cage day or night the prime dreamscape. Not just for weather, though he could be spun by a gust to catch what was bearing down, savor cloud plumes on parade, a storm driven his way that might miss him in a stately pirouette. It was the canvas scribbled with birds, hovering one at a time on high, or migrating long drooping lines, or swooping and soaring a myriad seized by one impulse. And at night, moon and planets, endless stars, their ancient patterns, chance sprinklings, clockwork. Perhaps defining both sanity and insanity, to lie on his back looking up, see what he could never touch, as close as living might approach the infinite. The sky was the spot he was in, the live predicament, the inverted translucent bowl sporting wisps and woollies, blue and gold with day or black with spangled night, or stormy inscrutable gray. With windows astonished whatever might come, sprung widest at sunrise and sunset.

WALKING THE BEACH BAREFOOT in the dark, letting the wavering wet line lap at him, the clown savored the moods of the sea. How it could command attention even in its sleep. How it played gently and rough with what lit on its surface. How it ground everything large and hard down to a gritty nothing. How it seemed to know things, whether respected or ignored, how it could snarl or turn prayerful hours or days before the big storm might arrive. How repetitive its dance moves, yet with those one-in-a-million upsets never boring, never bored. How with a supreme indifference it might stall, go cataleptic, settle down to a whisper, down to glass. How whatever washed ashore was never litter, but ornament, evidence, occasion, offering. How the one salt sea uncontained round the world was home, that he dreaded yet was drawn to, far inland found he missed, reminded how insular he'd been, how oblivious.

BUT COEVAL WITH WATER WERE the mysteries of earth, undulating, yawning underfoot and mounting up. How it spread the unmade bed of living, even at its harshest gathered nutrition to its clefts and fissures, broke open stones, broadcast weeds. How it welcomed being plowed and raked and manured, how it made new life of rot, how for years it waited, fairly begged for rain, drank all it could of what passed through, then let runoff bear away discarded signs of living. How it welcomed lovemaking and birth, the kinship of starry and planetary motions, the wake and sleep of sun and moon, with a drowsy nod and embrace in a drift of dry leaves welcomed death itself.

MESMERIZED HE WATCHED THE FIRE in the hearth in the night eat the logs, chuckle and hiss out its song—mindless and indifferent but not infantile, never demanding to be fed, content to spit and spark, build to a roar then settle back, slump to ashes that fell through the grate to a cooling bed at last. All-consuming, all-engrossing, the recital of its leaping hungers down to its pulsing embers spoke of fierce appetite, of loneliness and loss, of the winding down of the world, of what we were up against. Whether or not anyone kept vigil, it soon ate the wood whole, breathed out its song to warm the moment at the cost of those annular rings soft and hard, those tight-wound years past. Yet always he was moved to stir and prod it, keep it company, keep it going, feed it more.

THE BEAUTY OF NIGHT FOR THE NIGHT OWL was how doings spaced out in the quiet, didn't crowd one another, left room to rest the eyes and contemplate. Where each heartbeat and footstep landed separate, splashed through heart's shallow puddle, to ripple in night's deeper pool. Where the dark lent room for reflection, sorting feelings. You could tiptoe around the house, look in on the sleepers, tuck and straighten covers they'd kicked off, hear them sigh and snort and sweetly mumble, turn angry or serious, or get lost and plead with someone likewise tumbled in the mind's dream nest. Among sleeping clowns the words a jumble, an earnest tone to the nonsense, the brow knitting then smoothing itself.

THE LATE-NIGHT CLOWN THOUGHT one great evolutionary enigma must be moths. He had seen moths immolated by open fires, unable to resist the allure. Before electricity how did they do their nightly dance, part mosh pit and part pattycake? It must be a fatal attraction, drawn as they were to campfires and torches, to forest fires and range fires that outran the antelope. Or in olden times had there arisen a smarter subtler moth, wary of heat, who did his courting by Saint Elmo's Fire and foxfire, or by the full moon's light? Even so, wouldn't the party cry out for a beacon, the lovers a roar of inspiration, the dance a fevered spark?

HE WAS GIVEN A PAIR OF TICKETS to the season's final game. The team was in the basement, with no hope of making the playoffs. He called everyone he knew, and at least some were frank, said they couldn't stand to watch those hopeless losers once more. But what was ever hopeless but a future preordained? The day dawned bright but cold, and he got there early enough to dispose of the ticket—but there were no takers, and none of the usual scalpers. He left the ticket at the window, made the seller promise to give it away. Inside, with that empty seat alongside he watched the game sag downhill to the final whiff and smack, in this wan milky light slurped the last of his beer, pocketed the dregs of his peanuts, shuffled out in the gathering dark. The losing home team hadn't played with much heart, with nothing at stake but a paycheck, preoccupied with their rest. Yes, it was only a game, but what you made of it made you, what you gave it gave you back.

ASTONISHING HOW MUCH OF the so-called formative years, that first handful where he learned to walk and talk, use a toilet, climb, laugh, run, play games—some of the hardest lessons passed before he was even aware. As they did for his siblings and kids. Aside from confused pain and terror, what made things stick in memory? What forced the young mind wide-awake, besides loss, rage, jealousy, fear? This side of the divide it seemed a gentle, trusting upbringing might prolong naïve oblivion, encourage self-erasure.

OF COURSE HE DIDN'T KNOW what he didn't know, a conundrum, a tautology. But then there was the hunch, the guess. The bluff and call. That mysterious leap in the dark, from body to mind to spirit the spark. What he didn't know began with the birth accident, with who that couple was, what they thought they knew and felt. Sure, we all set out as babies, and if lucky lay helpless awhile at the heart of a wordless affection. But then what? The ride started off with a lurch, and but for wheels on gravel, without the ghost of a clue. Then he was alternately taught or preyed upon or made things up till sense was begat out of nonsense, till something caught on what was what.

EVEN AS A KID HE ADMIRED alligator paint on old woodwork, palimpsest signs on brick walls with ghosts of old signs peeking through. Rock posters, circus posters, billboards pasted over, scraped off countless times, phone poles bristling with nails and staples and torn corners aflutter, nattering bygone announcements. This layering seemed both sloppy and intentional, the effect of a hasty present slapped on a deepening past that couldn't help but bleed through. It was comforting to see how last year and last century and all those gone before never quite went away, held on not just in graveyards and junkyards, but in fencerows and byways, in barn lofts, attics and alleys hung around. Iron rings to hitch teams to curbstones in the oldest parts of town. And the hype, the hyperbole? For all its shouting in the moment, the sales pitch yellowed overnight, appeared quaint and quiet next morning. When the tent came down, the flattened grass sprung back.

THE CLOWN REMEMBERED ONE WORD lettered on the front door to an old store that clutched at him till he felt possessed. The front part of the word leaned forward, an ornate italic, while the second part leaned back. In gold leaf on green it said En/trance. And indeed he was purely entranced. Years later he still wondered why he never walked through that door, why he stood there rejecting its invitation, why he had no clue what that opening offered and meant. Maybe it was like women so lovely they threatened one's life—their presence for the moment stopped the heart, and stole away the breath.

HE KNEW THE FOOTSTEPS OF LOVE often led to despair, but not the why and wherefore. And was it so inevitable? Many things on this wobbly earth were cyclical, how the light rose and fell, came and went, how tides retreated and returned, seasons sagged in mock despair and uplifted a pantomimed hope. So the living diverted by change rode out storms that both soothed and buffeted. And love partook of Heisenberg's Indeterminacy Principle, that bespoke how no one could measure the measure he moved to, while danced in its feathery grip. So love might persist and abide, the sight for sore eyes, its illusion the gift that kept giving even as life all around him gave and took.

WHAT WAS BETWEEN THEM WAS LIKE a cup set out in the rain to be filled by a rainy world without plumbing, that must have its occasional dry spells, even as its overflowing. True, some in time set out the cup upside down, their thirst a plain show of despair. If one were caged he might die of the lack, zen monk resigned to happenstance to fill the cup. But in this chancy watery world both were at liberty, of their own choice came and went. And the cup could always refresh them, yield them both delight, astonishment.

THERE WERE WOMEN WHO LOVED CLOWNS, couldn't help themselves, drawn to the pratfalls and lostness, the lyrical shame and oblivious wide blinking stares. Because truly what else was there, who else held you so long then released you so lovingly as a clown. It was like the craving for circus peanuts fresh roasted, that you shucked underfoot by the handful, gobbled while still warm. Left a litterbug trail worse than Hansel and Gretel. He didn't really want to be one of those famed for the taking and leaving, for the messy heart in its ill-fitting clothes, its silly wink and a wave, but sometimes that's who showed up in the morning, who wandered in after dark and eased into bed alongside.

HE ALWAYS THOUGHT HE READ BOOKS, went to galleries, films, plays, museums with the same excuse he roamed the world, to know more of life, live more lives. To savor all the tastes and differences. It was not a literal quest, or he'd have been content with zoos and prisons, with official categories, abrupt diagnoses and dismissals, recipes, menus, statistics. He was looking for what mattered, not what made for shades of preference, but what in its endless variety made humans and their world all one. He went places to put himself there, to negotiate those conditions. To meet other sailors waiting out the weather for a passage, for the waves to die down, the wind to come around. Or the heart to rise in the night, button up the boat and go for it.

TO HAVE LIVED MORE LIVES THAN ONE was not just to have lived and remembered. There was the living itself, then equally inexplicable, the sharing living. Which was the province of both loving and art, art a kind of ghostly loving wider than one's arms. Where doubts could be won over by connections newly made. And however loving spun poems, novels, films, plays into being, it was begun with a dance, an arabesque of voice and body, a dash and chatter of brush strokes that fingered the blushing dawn before it could lapse into day. Living might regret things left undone, mount vast fevered dreams in the night, waken longings, even stalk autumn thickets, crush underfoot its own husks. But both loving and art conjured the impossible, summoned chimeras to stand in the place of experience, in that forest clearing over an open fire render the stuff of living into a piquant sauce to flavor one's personal portion, spice one's dreams.

SO IN THE END THERE WERE THOSE who might never possess a lover in the flesh, or not for long, might live a whole life in that faltering half-light. Might learn instead how fashioning art could make one irresistible as a mayfly yet as momentary, as expendable along the dappled stream. And how having a lover lifelong might cost both too much and too little. How, flawed as it couldn't help but be, the ghostly living on might prove the best one could possibly mean, though that might be a secret kept even from one's stoical or grieving conscious self.

YET FRIENDS OFFERED VACATIONS, diversions. They forgave his missteps in their dances not quite spelled out. With a wobbly folding chair set in their lives, he could watch and kibitz all he wanted, these weren't his cards being played. Of course some friends were just lovers you didn't sleep with, avoiding that subtle confusion, the promise of who was whose and what what. Friends could be like family, aunts and uncles and siblings, that exasperatingly close. He'd known clowns who cleared the deck of friends and relations the moment they found romance or hit the bigtime, as if anyone near and dear in the hard old days must be tainted. And back in the Depression, folks went to extremes—either took in rabbit-poor friends and relations or shunned them completely, disencumbered made a show of going it alone.

TRULY NO ONE COULD LIVE WITHOUT LOVE, even if it were only a dog or cat petted by her steady source of kibble. Or one's own love in art's funhouse mirrors reflected back on oneself. Some small helpless ones perished of their parents' resentment, indifference, neglect, while others were rescued by outsiders who upheld and fed them. Splendid-coated Joseph dropped down a well by his brothers was rescued by strangers, baby Moses plucked out of bulrushes was raised up by a queen. Men on Death Row got marriage proposals from pen pals who would not leave them alone to meet their unmaker. A few had more compassion, could more easily see that essential kinship through the thin guise of another, though many hearts, perhaps hardened by the bubblegum snap of success, turned to stone.

HE WAS TRYING TO RECALL his last uncontrollable laugh, when the peals tumbled out until the tears came. So rare, they should be more memorable. What had it been about? He thought you had to be holding your gut a certain way, braving the present moment with no hope of reinforcements, no relief. The boy on the burning deck, Roland with his trusty Durendal at Roncevaux. Yet you couldn't be alone, such laughter fed on itself; the brushfire demanded fuel, strong wind, a spark. That zinger an absurdity so vast it stunned analysis. So no little puzzles, wordplay, clever jibes and japes. A tap to the funnybone out of the blue, and not with some doctor's pert rubber hammer, but a croquet mallet. Your buddy looking fierce says "Where's that twenty you owe me—cough it up." And you cough, and he laughs, then you're both coughing and laughing, in the grip of something racketing like a freight train through you both.

HE WONDERED AT AND SAVORED humor's powers. In the grip of the serious and rational, the rat race of winners and losers that threatened sanity and health, what he craved was a mindset that found things funny, prolonged laughter that conjured a release. The laugh that touched the latch, that freed the bird from its cage. What launched the brain vapor could be immaterial, sometimes a slip of the tongue, a hiccup or tickle. Any nudge to the mind that expected the world to make sense, that rejected despair at the meaningless, instead found itself swept up in a cleansing rush. Where did Putin hide his armies? Up his sleevies.

HARDEST WAS FINDING A WAY INTO the comic free-fall free-for-all, getting past the wind resistance that snatched at you, brought you whistling to earth for a face-plant. It was hard catching your own self off-guard, letting the carefree overwhelm the careful for even a two-count. So you started griping about the weather, recalled a funny fight phrase like spitting chiclets, told a joke, then another, then piled them on like flapjacks past the point of surrender. Say, it looks like you're eating for two. Two, you say? I'm eating for an army, want to grow into a target they can't miss until the tears came, till the illogic of feelings climbed aboard and started surfing until everything got funny, waves rolled on and on. Because otherwise it was hopeless, this humorless clodhopper case of the blues groaning about his bad knees on a concrete trampoline, still jumping up and down.

BUT THEN HE SUSPECTED SOME OF THOSE who laughed loudest might have no sense of humor at all. Were often angry or disappointed creatures boxed, nailed shut, living their whole lives in lockdown. Pretending amusement at the world, theirs could be at best a hollow laugh, a sarcastic dismissal, as if to say what amuses is worthless, beneath contempt. An excess of laughter might come upon one in a stretch of lostness, of hysteria, of drought believing rain would never come. And humor was a houseplant you had to feed and water, or take out and stick back in the dirt. When he told such folks a joke, one that tested their gut response to living's incongruities, say about finding a loaded baby diaper in a toilet right when you had to go, he might be met with baffled stares, then an artificial roar. Though on an off-night he might not be all that funny. And unless they had little clowns at home not potty-trained, they might be way too polite.

SO A SENSE OF HUMOR WAS A BLESSING, balm to a life lived beyond one's control, as a cog in the machine. Shaved ice to the burning tongue. When you felt truly footloose, the ploy might be drugged incoherence, an oblivious stroll to the crumbling edge, letting the conscious mind lurch and flop like a baby. Knowing that even in full possession of your powers you could not affect outcomes you most desired could lend a certain lift, a levity. Why bother asking who your children might turn out to be, who your parents were before you turned up in their lives? Like dark grownup dreams of flying, you knew too much to close your eyes and dive into a martini. Yet stone serious living some days was dropping down a well, with no room to pop a chute. At least once you made a joke you felt that jerk.

SO THERE WAS SAVAGE HUMOR THAT BIT the crippled leg, and gentle humor that fluffed up the pup for a pillow. But all at once the clown realized he loved the jokes of a world that had never been yet still might come to be, far more than the world he'd been given. He was tired of jokes full of cultural and racial and sexual stereotypes, where the rabbi got the worst or the best of it, or the blonde or the Irishman. So this wombat walks into a bar, and asks the bartender if his dad has been in today. And the bartender says I don't know, what does he look like?

THEREBY THE CLOWN GREW DEFINITE, playful yet serious, neither denying the other. Straight face for joking, grin for the dark heavy matter. Jibes like a shake of the reins and click of the tongue to stir the drowsy team to step ahead. So deeply set in his life, yet some days so lightly risen, roused from a nest in a thicket, heaved up off the damp ground, set forth into the day on the same compass heading he'd been on when he lay down. Accepting that clowns could be anyone, intensely silly and voluble about things no one else cared about. Like where spotted owls liked to nest or how to clean a dirty river or what mules thought. He might spend half a day considering whether eating pies were ever meant to be thrown, or the point of his one grandma's frilly postcard collection, or how the painted turtles in his kids' terrarium got named Dante and Plutarch.

THE CLOWN WAS SICK. Down with fever, chills, delirium. But then he woke thinking the clown was the sickness, not him. Just as for some the clown was infancy, or teen rebellion, the first real job, serious steady drinking, the onset of responsibilities, even retirement and old age with its finicky neatness, its ruffles of irrelevance. That the clown could be hardness of hearing, a routine where you got everyone to shout rudely what they'd just said politely. Which come to think of it made misunderstanding the clown. Which might be lethal if it had a badge and gun. And here he only had the sniffles, a hot dry throbbing forehead and a craving for chocolate mint ice cream, that he kept being out of, since he refused to write it on the list, since lists were for the brain-dead. A goose honk when he blew his nose? Things could be a whole lot worse.

THE CLOWN'S EARS BUZZED AND ROARED from working and playing as a boy around things going full blast. Craving to get as close to the speaker or jack hammer as he could, to run equipment without muffler or earplugs, feel the pulsing rock band churn his innards to jelly. Now a mysterious blessing of the morning walk through fields and woods was the still of his own ears, that in the cool air quieted, let him savor birdsong trills and tremolos, hear the trees creak and sigh, twigs and leaves underfoot pop and crackle, without adding their fizzy cacophony.

EARLY ON HE LEARNED HOW THE BODY broke down, wore out. How you pounded nails, pounded dirt, pounded steel till your elbows couldn't take it, your shoulders wrists and knuckles gave out, your ankles hips and knees. So old clowns had to work slower and smarter or not at all. Had to warm up and cool down, keep their balance. Like the old ones said, you needed to start using your head—though where did that get you? For a lot of clowns the head was just a different hammer. So was the wallet for that matter, and that other head in the pants.

ON HIS 60TH BIRTHDAY, a rainy blustery spring day, the clown was thrown a surprise party aboard an old tall ship docked in Lake Union. The Wawona was a logging schooner with three masts stripped of rigging, with not much else now but bow and stern lines, gangway and bilge pump. That leaky moldering ship had long been half a ghost, emptied of bunks, stove and sails, of her captain's sextant and log, of her chronometer, ship's bell and weather glass. Now covered with scaffold and plastic to keep weather out while being worked on, her identity simplified to scarred deck and damp hold, she was a metaphor afloat, a huge buoyant emptiness. Yet here a jolly crew gathered, played music, danced and made merry, wide-eyed, uplifted a moment, feeling joined and embarked, conscious what that meant. How one's life might as well be a boat, a chance to traverse the abyss, to nod at catastrophe, move on the wind at a whisper, make one's way from one unknown port to another, and given the luck of the draw make that passage in rare company.

IT WAS CLEAR BY NOW TIME WAS nobody's playmate: voracious, relentless, inexorable. Never mind licking names off tombstones like they were scribbled icing, time ate the whole cake if it sat too long. Ate that granite lump in the freezer, without a silver fork or proper manners,

126

without even ice cream. And time was forgetful, didn't know or care whose birthday it was. Went marching on through light and dark, thick and thin. But then time was also nature's way of avoiding collisions, of sorting things out, of keeping everything from going off at once, like the next Big Bang. Though that wasn't much consolation to those who made use of brakes and a steering wheel. Who, when they saw something dangerous coming, didn't just hug the airbag.

IN ONE BAKERY THE CLOWN LOVED they didn't scrape off messages and names from cakes ordered but never picked up. They just put a red tag on each, and lowered the price, knowing somewhere right this moment an impromptu party was gathering, that like time itself would buy any excuse, and eat up every crumb.

THE WOOD-CARVING CLOWN KNEW most folks these days if they carved anything besides tofu turkey worked linoleum and that stuff they made countertops with. If they worked in wood they didn't mess with runout or ripples, with tigerstripe, birdseye or quilt. It was machined in fancy jigs with precision motors, tungsten carbide blades. A CNC machine could turn out an F model mandolin scroll without your risking a fingernail. But the grain they avoided and ignored was the direction living took, its free-form self-support, held still all its tensions and strivings, its swirling subtle as a night wind through a pine grove. Yet fixed in place the tree's grain fought storms and beetles, misery whip, ax and lightning, told in each chip what was left of its life, of its fat years and lean in a soft and hard layered story. Each tale of resistance, reach and flow asked that the maker's tool follow its living a little, even slip, make concessions, take pains. Find in a knot what the wood had to say, what it wanted to say all along, of wars and waste, of phantom limbs.

MIRED IN TIME HE FOUND ONE SALVATION, one physical immortality, in how some instruments just got better with age. Especially wooden ones—fiddles, cellos, pianos, guitars. It came from the nature of trees, their long lives bent to invisible forces and sprung back. You wanted to steer clear of dolled-up plywood beaters, born dead to stay dead, clunky discouragements to frighten kids off making noise. But if humans kept playing the ones built right from the start, the very attributes of age—fragility, immediacy, plain speech, responsiveness—might somehow be raised to a power. Instruments could age like fine brandies in casks, might grow smoother for centuries. The voice in each over time sung ever louder and truer, opened clear to the heart at long last.

IN THE 60S SOME ROCKERS PLAYED like it was Armageddon, hammered the bloody flaming stump to sparks, then smashed their instruments. And when the buzz wore off, bought new ones. Then there was Willie Nelson, who picked a hole right through the top of his guitar but didn't fix it or toss it, just kept sounding better. The clown once bawled out a big-city painter who had broken a handmade guitar to paint a still life that was all about his needy violence. The clown had never seen an ax worthy of being trashed, no matter how crummy, nor one so worn out a tune couldn't be coaxed from it.

BY RIGHTS THE CLOWN'S SOUNDTRACK should have been a brass band or steam calliope, at the very least a solo on slide trombone to a patter of softshoe and slapstick. Some days he danced barefoot, singing Grab your coat, forget your hat, leave your worries on the doorstep. Splashed through Singing in the Rain. Then there were days that dragged, when he sang Take Dis Hammer and Old Rugged Cross in his mud-caked boots, where he had to watch his toes, where everything lifted got dropped. Then at last, gray-haired as a blind baker on graveyard shift, his days waltzed to the sighing of wind in the pines, the chuckle of gutters and downspouts, of birds who sang only their names, phoebe, bobwhite and whippoorwill, to a backbeat of woodpeckers, mourning doves, owls. Dance moves essential as always, since in costume with red nose and makeup the clown was wordless, dumbstruck.

AND WHAT WAS MUSIC ANYHOW but silences between notes, a backhand invisible measure? Rhythmic counter to both presence and absence, both stillness and cacophony. The clown found playing music the ultimate sanity. He'd started playing with others for something to do at parties, to damage himself less, since the songs and tunes lent him a joyful feeling, no matter how sad what they said. And while the song lasted time stood still. Once players found its groove, the tune felt like it could go on forever. Sad or happy, playing conjured a presence he felt part of, that erased all desire to be elsewhere. And if at the end of the day he sat and played, just let the fingers wander, he'd soon learn what he had left to go on, and what the day's work had meant.

THEN THERE WAS MUSIC AND MOTION. He'd started playing guitar, slide and mandolin to the motion and sway of the trains, the low-down clatter and squeal of tracks and wheels, the clanging and horns at grade crossings, syncopating the rhythm that carried him, that drove the music for hours. Riding on the City of New Orleans, Casey Jones, Wabash Cannonball. Too bad they didn't still run those vintage dome cars with their grand acoustics. And when he set sail, especially out of sight of land, the sea raised all that sway, surge and patter to a power. Out on the Rolling Sea Where Jesus Speaks to Me, What Does the Deep Sea Say, Drifting Too Far From the Shore.

FINALLY HE FELT JOINED TO MUSIC as to a river, like the Ganges that fingered and sung out its thousand mouths to the sea. How, clear or murky, fresh or brackish or salt, in its myriad voices it was all one. How you could start anywhere, classic or country, symphony or lullaby, and find yourself trying to play and sing some other distant part, felt like you were chipping a corner off its blue iceberg to fill your cup. How you picked up some things in passing like burrs that stuck to you, not because you studied or learned them, but because they answered an attraction, knew they were taken in, felt. Knew that your path was where their seed should drop. And how there was no one way to do it or feel it or share it, how its changes resisted control, how there was music you loved so clearly yours, bobbing in the backyard wading pool, and music that you loved so far beyond you, that foamed ashore still singing of the depths.

FOR THE CLOWN MUCH OF THE WORLD was a bowl, not a ball. He felt drawn to and held by wherever he was, even if he only touched down for days or hours. Whether it was the gold country along the American River, the clamorous jungles of Panama, the narrow cobblestones of the French Quarter, or the wooded stone mountains of New Hampshire, he felt a pull to some center that bid him linger, obliquely ask of folks what their lives were hereabouts. Otherwise he was on the move out at the rim, where things wobbled around, unsettled without and within.

ROVING THE WORLD HE CONSIDERED homecoming and exile, wondered if he even had a home outside the mind compelled to live by itself. If he'd gotten further from home when he was growing up, would it have made any difference? His folks didn't want him anywhere else, they traveled to escape him along with the others, needed him to help anchor and manage the crowd of little ones they had left. So the first time he got a few hundred miles from home it was under his own power, with no one else's knowledge or consent. When he finally chose a school on his own, the one that would pay him a little was furthest off, over mountains clear out to the coast.

FOR THE TRAVELING CLOWN there were two movements—going out into the new, and touching the familiar heading back. He always felt that click of the frog in the switch, where the curve became a loop, where overt adventure ended, when like it or not he had fallen into his own outbound footsteps back-tracked to his tame, tethered self. Then too the moment came on long trips when exploration flattened out, when new places began to look alike, unexciting, and had no more to offer. When for the moment the variety of existence had worn thin, when this wandering felt like stalling, like putting off what was still in him waiting back home to be done.

TRAVELING IT SEEMED HE'D ALWAYS KNOWN the difference between a journey and a trip. Long before the advent of mind-altering drugs, a journey was a pilgrimage, hidden or overt, best pursued in humble guise, anonymous, hoping for an awakened heart and mind, a change of self. Ready for anything, the pilgrim slept in his clothes, close by his shoes, hat and staff. The journey that returned you unexpanded was a flop. By contrast a trip was an indulgence, an excursion, a funhouse ride to the interior, surgically quick, where you knew what awaited you at the poolside bar and come-as-you-are restaurant, with fresh towels and linens and on your pillow and sometimes in your hair a chocolate mint. Because who that can afford it is not worth it. The tripper had to be back in harness Monday morning, didn't expect a new and different person to wake up ignorant of where to call in sick. And the spirit hated to ride herd on a fleshy self-indulgence, craved to be up on the dusty coachbox with the driver riding shotgun, where both could spit and cuss, and see at a distance what's what.

THE SAILOR CLOWN LOVED ISLANDS, where people endlessly
climbed aboard and splashed ashore, worked and played within lim-
its, sat down and held onto boats. It was good to work with what was
at hand, like a cook clean the catch of the day, eat what was in season
and grew here. Besides which, islanders were realistic, felt the need for
buoyancy, knew planes and cars had their limits. If water was four-fifths
of the skin of the planet, then life around water represented sanity, a
primary adjustment to its damp reality. With its isolation and slow pace
an island might help concentrated effort and dalliance, mingled work
and play, as it drew a line in the sand round the self.

AT SEA THE MIND MET WITH subtle complications, turned back
as it was on itself. Here change was ceaseless, unrelenting, came splash-
ing over him, waves thrown aloft like snowflakes, no two identical.
Yet the mindless heave and lurch soon dissolved all sense of novelty,
and with everything and nothing to look at, the mind was both fretted
and lulled by a surface sameness that challenged identity, and drained
relevance. As with the gear, the blocks and lines, the sails and their stout
stitchery, given all this motion something in the mind could rub till it
wore through.

SOME DAYS HE THOUGHT others deluded, confused about where
they were, which way they were headed, trusting mangled GPS coordi-
nates. After all, for security reasons the NSA could switch all those satel-
lites off in a heartbeat, and then where were we? Not to mention how,
but for holidays spent meandering, location plus direction plus time
equaled one's living identity. Forget DNA scans and Facial Recognition
software, the only way to navigate one's way in the scheme of things was
presence, contact, the touch through the fog at arm's length. Otherwise
it was all a dark grope, a bump and grind to a halt, everyone in the
gloom so much waterlogged furniture.

THE CLOWN NAVIGATED MOSTLY by means of Bowditch's Dead
Reckoning and John Keats's Negative Capability. He also thumbed
a rough-and-ready treatise called Lifeboat Navigation. Rule One was
make your best guess where you were, then guess where you might want

to be. Passive, observant, alert and practical, which mostly meant literal-minded, on land or sea he leaned back, let the way talk to him. Once in a while he ran aground, admitted he was lost, begged directions from a local, asked which way to the nearest landmark. But secretly he didn't care—he was in it for the ride. He knew to watch which way he spat. And when he looked out to hold onto his hat.

GOING TO AND FRO OVER THE EARTH and its waters, he saw one message in everything living and inert, stillborn or swollen in the womb of night—that change was the action of time and chance, whether random turmoil or steady drip. For 4.6 billion years, time the patient idiot picklock tried one thing then another, to breach every barricade, dissolve every structure, steal every succulent. The planet heaved in its long slumber till the arrival of so-called intelligence. Then man the marauder tomb-raider outran time itself, to feed his widening appetites took all in a relative instant on an unchecked shopping spree. No telling where he might turn next, from beaver pelt hats and fricasseed passenger pigeons to oil rigs over the North Pole. Perfecting the planet's exhaustion. And for what? For an orgasm of conquest, for a black hollow laugh.

STILL, GROWNUPS PLANNED THEIR ESCAPES. Some even made first-class reservations, but then mum's the word till they got to the gate, whipped out the pass, lifted off. The eternal child saw a gap in the fence and a light in the distance that beckoned, so wiggled through, and till it was time for bed never once looked back. But the clown? The clown knew nothing of planning, and snagged on a nail ripped his pants. Got caught and stayed caught till he was practically naked. Then unfurled a foolish manic flag to cover his public parts.

WALKING THE STRAIGHTEST GENTLEST TRAIL up the valley, the clowns crossed one dry crickbed then another several times, that left them dryshod as they dipped into its groove and climbed back out again. In its bed limestone stairsteps jumbled, upended, signs of great force, long patience, indifference or neglect. But signs of water too in the few shaded pools, in the stately sycamores that marched along the banks, that would never stray from this dry bed that promised a deep soaking several times a year. Water ran off these hills, ran away from a thirsty green that hung on through droughts all summer, waiting to drink a downpour.

THERE WAS A LITTLE WHITE FURRY ANIMAL on the tractor tire they had jacked up and were methodically turning, looking for the source of the leak, the usual thorn or nail. The clown put on his glasses to see this fuzzy dab or smudge the size of a grain of wheat, traveling on what seemed to be its thousand legs. Then it fell off, landed on the chunk of wood the jack was resting on. His brother went to get his camera and a pill bottle to put it in. But when the clown knelt to slide his knife blade under and lift the creature, it fell apart of its own weight, and the parts scurried off, disappeared into cracks in the plank. No telling what to make of its agreement as identity. He thought of a dragon in a Chinese New Year's parade, a fearful paper disguise that joined half the people there, that could hardly see itself, yet danced with great menace and glee.

THE CLOWN LIKED THE IDEA OF FRUITBATS stealing sweets in the night, liked the idea of chain-gangs that sang as they worked, through there might also be something in each to dislike. Young clowns would boldly declare what they hated: broccoli, spinach, brussels sprouts. Dirty windows. Dirty dishes. Flat tires. Bats awobble at twilight. And waiting for anyone anywhere, even at the other end of church for the wedding march over petals sprinkled by tiny fingers, shaken by the lowest organ notes. Hate like love had to be carefully parceled out. Enough to think what you liked while quietly tasting a little, keeping your opinions to yourself.

THE CLOWN'S YOUNGER SISTER WAS DYING, had inoperable lesions and tumors all over her brain. She was treated with radiation that gave her a few months—one more spring and summer to play. She flew to New Orleans, then took a riverboat north, a train west. Invited along friends and family. People then were talking about their bucket lists, which struck him as silly. Checking off things to be done while you could, lavish or challenging, gliding through exotic scenery while sipping rare vintages, as if the point of living were to rattle off a string of deathbed boasts, as if trying to convince even you you'd had enough. With her traveling done and the symptoms worsening she tried to kill herself, but failed when the medics appeared in two minutes, since she lived just across the road from the hospital. What then? The clown came for the rest of the ride, to spend what would be the last seven weeks with her. Picked and cooked all the ripening stuff in her garden. Picked guitar and sang around the kitchen table, while the pots bubbled. Picked some little rides through the neighborhood, pushed her in the wheelchair to some favorite spots, discovered some new spots together. Filling her days was easy. They kept it playful, gently silly. He did the insulin and blood checks for her diabetes, as he had when she was small. When it hurt they fixed the pain. She told stories of her twenty years on this spot, of how the deer used to come up the road from the woods, several times ate her garden to nothing overnight. She told about her nursing patients, how she treated terminal cases one at a time in their homes, how they waited and watched for her, saved up an earful to tell her. She told about her favorite watering hole, the scene of regulars there almost like a family, tried to say what that meant. How she'd almost like to be sitting on her favorite stool at Happy Hour this minute, then looked around and said Or maybe not.

IN HIS SISTER'S LAST MONTH the high point of her day might be the Ant Report. Every morning when she woke the clown would recite a list of official ant sightings in her bungalow while she'd slept. They seemed genuinely curious about their host, and could hardly be kept out of anything, so for them there were no secrets. These were tiny black members of a supercolony from the river banks of Argentina, Paraguay and Uruguay, stowaways aboard container ships bound north, that had settled 600 miles of California coast. There were also supercolonies on permanent vacation in the Med and in Japan. Unlike ordinary ants limited to a radius of 56 feet from the nest, who fought rivals to the death, Argentine ants roamed widely and played nice. Having mastered the secret of cooperation, these transcendent ants would soon rule the universe. He found them in her garage sipping spilled antifreeze, bushwacking the thicket of her hairbrush, strolling the dark side of the mirror in her medicine cabinet, studying her heaps of useless meds in ziplock bags, exploring her mysterious array of sparkly socks.

CONFUSED WAS THE CLOWN'S DYING SISTER on the drugs for the tumors that had her brain and body in their grip. No more time now no parade but all at once it came at her, ran through her and spilled forth. Hers a quiet voice still the love song of a lovely instrument, though the words all uncoupled their stories now all one. Yet even so, something joyous to the lilt the race and tumble, the arc of these broken pieces in mid-air. And no matter how fast they came, how scattered, since he'd helped raise her and teach her to talk he mostly caught her shorthand on the wing, mostly could tell what she meant. Sing harmony, nod and smile back.

THE MORNING SHE DIED in a blinding burst, an abrupt rush and lapse to nothingness, her body was cleaned and prepared for the funeral home by her oldest dearest nurse friend. Then that woman performed one more office. She took a plastic bucket and poured in every pill and medicine, more than a gallon of them, then mixed in some soupy stuff that hardened all these unused and still dangerous meds into a worthless blob that couldn't seduce or distract or harm anyone. Its congealed sludge once dream clouds meant to fog pain, conjure hallucination, court oblivion. Too bad, since they had cost thousands. But better this than the pollution of flushing down a toilet or burning in a backyard barbecue. Or a stray someone swallowing.

HE HAD NEVER KNOWN ANYONE who quite owned the secret of living deeply and fully, every minute. But in her final weeks his sister had come close. Could her capacity for joy have been enhanced by her surrender? Whatever her secret, it had to be held lightly. Never mind dying, most folks had weightless stretches where they felt like a dry dandelion about to be dispersed. For a while he thought the secret was love—how it put the shine and edge on living, lent weight and significance to a touch, but then simmered down, wore off. When you had done all you could to keep it hot and bright, there you sat lost as ever. Playing music helped, and juggling, and telling jokes that made fun of no one—always harder than it looked. People were such huge easy targets, tethered to truck bumpers like balloons in an Easter parade, ponderously nodding down at kids armed with popguns, taking aim.

THE SEASONS CAME ROUND AND ADVANCED, leapt up, leafed out, flowered and fruited, then slumped back to rest—so things kind of returned but not quite. Not a circle, more a loopy spiral. Loves like tidal ebbs and flows were still not the selfsame love you declared eternal. Because storm-tossed, muddied then clarified, people changed, patience eventually worn thin as the soles of their favorite shoes. So what we had was what abided in us, what lingered, maybe treasured in a prominent out-of-the-way spot of honor like the mantel, or hidden beneath the ordinary in a dresser drawer. Or parked in weeds like one's first car that had long since come to rest, too much trouble to dispose of, break back down to its elements, place-marker and reminder wearing on past death at its own rate, upholstery stolen for birds' nests, crazed and cloudy windshield once transparent, seen through anyhow, framing the leisurely unwinding way ahead.

EVERY PLANT BEGAN LIFE AS A WEED native somewhere, so much at home its life seemed effortless. All weeds had strategies to outreach, outrun, outclimb competitors. Blackberry led creeper and ivy a season-long chase. Who could keep up with wild grape, hops, morning glory, tumbleweed? Some poisoned the ground of their enemies, as tulip and daffodil were rumored to treat each other. Some like maple launched whirligig seed to escape the shade of their parents. Some shared seed as food for other creatures, so squirrels might bury more nuts than they could remember or need. Some hid their seed in fruit to be eaten and shat out by birds miles away. Some favored the extremity of fire, that opened their cones, released seed on charred ground purged of rivals. Successful weeds over time roamed far and wide. With the aid of tribes selecting and trading seed over thirteen thousand years, tomatoes spread from Central America up into Maine and Canada. Likewise corn and squash, peppers and beans spread north, west and east from where someone first bravely tasted, then pocketed seed for the ride.

THESE DAYS THE EARTH STILL SEEMED all one. Place, season, climate, the clown felt hardly one to judge. Foods had little hold on him, or beds—though he was thankful touching what he ate, where he tumbled and slept. What he was most curious about were people and the other animals, those most skilled and easygoing, most durable, most alive to the feathery tips. Those who paraded possessions and accomplishments left him cold. At the same time he understood the power of home, where one's tools lay sharp at hand, where sudden needs could be met, things done without fuss in a moment, taken up right when things broke or inspiration struck. Yet he saw how birds abandoned the nest without a thought the instant child-rearing was done.

SELF-KNOWLEDGE WASN'T ALL it was cracked up to be. It had taken half a life to gather this paltry bundle that was still a mess to unpack. But something had to convince you to get out of bed in the morning, come up with a plan not just a stall till something better knocked. And drunk or no drunk you still had to brush your teeth before bed, if you wanted teeth in the morning. Which was not a given, what with soft-boiled eggs, pudding and room service. But for most of us like it or not there were things like teeth in your life, routine and matter-of-fact, that could take the fun out of breakfast. Necessities like air in your tires, oil in your crankcase, dirt in your flowerpot.

YET AT TIMES FOR HIM EVEN THE SUBJECT of discourse and tone of voice could be distractions from the being floating free—matters juggled round the kitchen table overdressed. Staring down salt and pepper and napkins, forks and spoons. Wishing the knife had more edge. Sometimes out in the dark swamp he wanted even the presence of the voice to fall away and greet the silence, let night's caterwaul withdraw, let its chirping and humming steal close. There he craved no melodic diversions or rasping distractions, no idiosyncrasies, nothing but the felt life deepening into the here and now, the full moon compelling that inner tide, upwelling the blood, inspiring expiring each breath.

SO IN LEAGUE WITH INVISIBLE POWERS he favored winds, tides, currents, the veiling and unveiling of the overheated planet in her fitful diaphanous striptease, the breathing out and in of dirt and plants and leaves, of waters brackish, salt and fresh, of reefs and hives, of hamlets and principalities of creatures miniscule and microscopic, burrowing from the light or swarming toward it, busy enduring and thriving. Then too came magnetism, gravity, solar winds and waves, and beyond subtle physical forces the range of the mind at work—of calculation, intuition, forethought and afterthought. And no less vital to explore and embellish living boundaries—singing and dancing and play.

THE CLOWN KNEW DEPRESSION was like being alone in a storm at sea. His job to outlast this rough patch that would exhaust itself eventually. He needed to dog the hatches and drive around chuckholes, quarter foam-topped barricades. Even in the endless heaving gray-on-gray, keep an eye peeled for weather and obstacles. Keep the habit of eating and drinking, even if he threw it right back up. Maybe at the worst admit exhaustion—set a sea anchor, tie down the tiller, strike the sails and go below. Wedge himself in a bunk with lee boards in an attitude of rest, a prayer that rest come visiting. And on deck hold the helm, trim the sails, harness himself to the boat, which was living, which may be the best of him a little damp inside and scoured without, but still afloat, on the move.

FOR THE HIGHEST AND LOWEST TIDES in over 30 years, he rose at first light from his bunk. Cup of tea in hand he drowsed on deck, watching the ancients being summoned—old growth cedar and fir lodged far up the beach, still not rotted enough to lie still, lifted from shallow graves, carried off, swirled and waltzed round the bay, then on the next risen crest heaved ashore at a fresh resting place. All a sleepy bump and grind for the buoyant self, migrating toward the emptiness.

SINCE HE'D FIRST VENTURED OFFSHORE, his dreams of departure rarely included planes or trains or cars. Hardly even feet on trails. These most elemental dreams would begin on a small boat dock, uncleating figure-eights, tossing lines aboard, pushing off. False dawn or sunset or pitch dark, there seemed no other story but this slow, all-encompassing way to go in search of the world for oneself. Where the going was everything. As Socrates said, at some point one must load his little boat with all he has and all he might need for the voyage, then commit his boat to the waves, which is to say live his life.

BAREFOOT ON A MUDDY BACKROAD with his pants rolled up he studied the fabric of dreams, woven of scraps torn from the waking life. How dreams were idiosyncratic, a personal apparatus cobbled to amuse, inform, encourage and frighten oneself even at rest. The dreamer was always engaged, felt its stream full-force like a fire hose played over his skin, that roared through and past him. The ride both active and passive, often lovely, seductive, sometimes scary, with no way to refuse but to open the windows, sit up, flail around, wrench oneself awake. Some dreams moved in advance of the workaday life, predictive as a daybreak flight of crows, where some were commentary from the dark wood of the past, night sounds mournful and vexed. The dreamer had to stand the shock of recognition at the familiar out of sequence and context, stand a harrowing fright at the mind's newly minted monstrosity. No matter, all conjure and conjecture, the rider amazed and astonished—by the sunlit familiar one instant, then back down the tunnel, by the mysterious, primal and profound.

BUT EVEN WIDE AWAKE WHAT SENSE could you make of a life that at its best and worst came rushing through you, over and past you like Niagara, that could not be stopped an instant, could not be slowed while the body made its demands, begged to be rested and fed? Yet some rare winters the great falls froze, its trickle in a death grip stilled. But not the life coursing through one, even sound asleep racing onward in its dreams.

NO ONE COULD RELIVE HIS WHOLE LIFE so that like art it was rendered compact, beautiful and true. No one could sing the swollen muddy river of her full experience, not Marion Anderson, not Maria Callas. Not even a twelve-fingered prodigy Mozart could scoop up and sound his short life. What one could do was fish that river and pull out an occasional denizen, a lunker perhaps once a lifetime—huge, gaping, goggle-eyed, hidden so long no one knew what to call it, what it fed on, whence it came. Considered as art at least you weren't asked to treat what you landed as sport or plaything, as dinner or catch-and-release. It could be a slapdash of song, sometimes a mute presence, sometimes a sleepwalking murderess with a bloody knife. The impossibility for the artist was to draw forth this monster and render it in the mind of another, vivid, freestanding, at large in its element.

AND WHAT OF THE STORY OF ART, of the pangs attending its birth, its despair and endless distractions, its snide ruthless jibes, its disruptions and discouragements? Yes, there was salvation to art, no matter how unpromising what it sometimes fed his life. It wasn't just therapy for untold injuries, nor medication for artist or audience, though that was how some mistook it. Art could summon a fearful random darkness, with at its center something flickering and unpredictable held in its focused beam. Art was living in this light of the mind and its feelings, through moments that became comprehensible, sometimes radiant with astonishment. Till what seemed a cure proved a joy.

BUT MAYBE LIVING OFFERED ONLY STORIES, nothing but. What else over time were folks left with but stories shared till familiar, that still drew a headshake, sigh or chuckle. What people did to each other, what they tried to prevent but did anyhow, what deals they made and broke, what they dreamt of then waked to do just the opposite—these fed life's wonder. Otherwise living was broken beads crunched underfoot, muttered loss. Otherwise it was a little love, a whole lot of beat-down, and a taste of the shared road, its mud mixed of dust and runoff. The stories couldn't contain, didn't bother to explain, merely possessed one a moment, showed another damaged in a ditch, baffled, lost, seeking to be found, gathering his wits.

YET WRITING COULD OFFER THANKSGIVING with extended family all gathered in one room. There were things said only to the person sitting alongside or across from him, things said to everyone in the room, at the big people's table and at the children's table, where things passed back and forth, always plenty to go around. There were even things said to the departed and to future guests, to everyone who ever sat in this room or who might sit here, should their day come. Stories of things as they were for some who might be right here, only decently disguised. Who's to say whose lives and doings these were, quietly borrowed and shared, whose lives had been or yet might be worth savoring, offered this moment afloat in the fullness of time.

THE CLOWN SUSPECTED THE NEW DOG that lived with them might be part coyote. She had the hairdo, size and look, and seemed a little too smart and knowing for her age, too independent. But then on a walk their first week or two, she tried to politely greet a big fluffy neighbor cat, who promptly jumped her. She yelped and split, where even a splash of coyote blood would have made lunchmeat of that house pet.

AND SHE BROUGHT OTHER MESSAGES he needed help with. For her daily walk he would sometimes take the dog past where they had found a freshly dead raccoon. A couple times a week she would dive into the bushes there and he would have to pull her off, so she wouldn't eat of the moldering slumped-in thing with its eyeless head turned from the light, its sharp teeth all agrin, despair or defiance no telling its final agony. By fall it was no more than a trampled rug, and he relented, let her sniff all she wanted, investigate with no fear she might savage its shredded collapsed little tent, locate and choke down its death. By the following spring she would still pause at the scent but they mostly passed by, pretended to ignore what had come to rest in these bushes, its scattered leavings hardly a place marker, that by now they both remembered and labored lightly to forget.

THE CLOWN SAW A LONG-DEAD FRIEND in a dream, looking jaunty as ever. In a crowded campus dining hall, where he was looking for a cup to make himself some tea at the boiling water spigot. The friend was below, down some steps, looking up when they spotted each other. The old friend seemed furtive, unsure. Then he said I couldn't go on like I was, I could see it coming, couldn't take the finish. He seemed to assume the clown knew what that meant, though he offered no clue. Do you kill yourself because of other people? Is there some profound or trivial knack to saving yourself for yourself? Then he realized his friend was with a couple of guys who were leaving. He grabbed his stuff—a bag, a coat, the tea in a ceramic cup—and jogged after them. They got on a train, a shiny new people-mover, but by the time he found somewhere to put his things, they'd disappeared. While it went lurching along in the dark, stopping, starting, he searched the train from end to end, asked the driver if the train looped back to where he got on, but he said I don't know, where did you get on? So he went back to where he'd put his stuff, took the cup of tea down from the overhead rack. It was half full and luke-warm. He finished it in a gulp, then woke.

THE MOMENT WAS DREAMLIKE, UPSETTING. The clown was under the back end of the car on a sunny afternoon, bleeding the brakes while his nephew pumped and held the pedal. Out of nowhere a thump hit the car. He heard his nephew say What the hell. He crawled out from

141

under and stood up. There was a dead crow at his feet, still warm, not breathing, not a mark on it, nothing ruffled or broke. Four other crows perched in the trees all around, hollering bloody murder. Do something, they seemed to shout. But what was there to do? He got a shovel and buried the crow in the garden while they watched. It seemed glossy and perfect, neither male nor female, neither old nor young. He laid it in the hole with the blade of the shovel, then sprinkled in a little dirt, that couldn't help but look wrong. There was no service, from the assembled mourners not a sound. Then his nephew said The crow just tumbled down from the sky, out of the middle of its life.

old clown

"Don't be afraid, the clown's afraid too." –Charles Mingus

SOMEWHERE IN THERE THE PACE picked up, the recent dozen years became a blur of train windows lit up in passing, gleam of an alley switchblade gone ere its tongue tasted blood. The bully Limited, hitting the horn for a crossing. Chuck Berry's phone-pole picket fence blown away by his hot-rod Lincoln. Time seemed no hay loft where you sat still enough to hear rustling lives all around, cooing, hooting, scampering. There were times to remember, grand moments, sure, but not embedded anymore in a workaday round of effort and accomplishment, hopeful plan flayed by exhaustion. No buckle to the belt that held your pants up, that felt like a strain and a burden. Suddenly here came suspenders, elastic waistbands, baggy pants to relax you, pledge comfort like it was salvation.

THE DESIRE TO SLOW THINGS DOWN and savor them had the perverse effect of speeding everything up. His 60s passed in a blur like an off-season vacation taken to avoid crowds, collisions with the familiar, expensive bedrooms and meals. He found himself alone in drenching rains, trudging storm-swept beaches, locked out of attractions closed for the winter that demanded ballooning new blue tarps for the moment, fresh coats of paint for later.

THREE 18-WHEELERS WERE PLAYING grab-ass tag down the mountain through light sprinkles, heading west into Cheyenne. The old clown in the right lane doing sixty saw them coming in the rearview round a bend. Two neck-and-neck strained to catch the one ahead, all three wide open, and there he was humming along in his blue tea-kettle, with a rocky median and steep dropoff to the right that left no running room. Then doing eighty or ninety they were on him: the leader by in a flash, then the other two on his bumper split apart, one taking the rumble strip down the clown's right, the other down his left, the tunnel of the two tight enough to brush wingtips. No point calling troopers, no spotting the tags on their rigs. Red and black and blue, in a heartbeat they tore past. Yet he was calm. He knew the madcap thrill of rule-breaking, had to admire this brush with the reaper, where a tap on the brakes by anyone meant a fishtail avalanche.

THIS TRIP HE NOTICED HOW produce trucks on Idaho freeways still didn't cover their loads. So at the moment in mid-September there were tons of yellow and white onions sprinkled on every upgrade and curve between Pocatello and Ontario. In a month there would also be spuds and field corn aplenty. This seemed either a time-honored tradition of largesse, or sign of a bone-deep laziness. He'd known a farmer who as a boy in the Depression looking for work had hitchhiked across Idaho, long before freeways. He said come fall no one would give him a ride, but there was always plenty to eat along the way.

THE WAY DEEPENED WITH THE YEARS, driving back and forth across the country since he'd first come west, found somewhere more homelike than home. Near half a century from those Ohio and Indiana hills, he'd passed through this harsh empty country, a fugitive in mountains and high prairie desert between where he'd been born and where he chose to be. Yet some of the way could also be lush and inviting, along the Platte and Green and Snake rivers, freezing or sweltering, with velvet skies shot with stars that made him pull over some nights, buffeted by the winds of others passing, to stand by the road staring up.

HE PULLED INTO THE FIRST REST STOP down out of the mountains. It was 3 am—he was overdue for a stretch and a nap. But when he went to the bathroom and brushed his teeth, there were these invisible people squatting and sitting all around, dark heads down, young and old, women and men, not one making a sound. Deliberately chewing tortillas, drinking from plastic jugs and jars, rolling newspaper cigarettes, whispering so faintly he couldn't catch a word. Thirty or forty ghost people whose breath wouldn't blow out a match, who pretended they were not watching, not watched, who shared what they had, passed around paper bags of dried fruits, chilis, carrots, who piled back into their vans and trucks without sounding a doorlatch, who pulled up tarps against the chill and didn't so much steal off as disappear.

144

THIS BAREFOOT YOUNG CLOWN was out in America, 3 am at a freeway rest stop talking to a buddy, girlfriend or boyfriend, brain-drooling into his cell phone. Indoors in an air-conditioned bubble, where the nightlife wasn't so loud, plugged into an outlet. When this groggy old clown stumbled into the building, the kid paused on his cell to say, Would you please step on that bug for me? It's freaking me out. So matter-of-fact, so polite. The old clown said It's only a June bug, they don't eat much, but gauging the young clown's hubcap eyes he stepped on it anyhow, felt token resistance, terminal crunch, and instantly regretted not saying Hang up and run for your life.

HE WOKE IN A REST STOP at sunup, and was shaving and brushing his teeth after a few hours' nap in the car. A man came in with a kid in pajamas and hung back after his boy ran out, leaned over and growled at him, "My boy shouldn't have to see that." Which he chewed instead of breakfast over the next hundred miles.

WALKING IN A PEASOUP FOG, hunched against the cold, a voice from behind burbled at him and a bicycle whooshed past. He never caught more than a wisp, but the voice was musical as a bird call, out of sight before he figured what she'd even said, though he could have scored and played its climbing notes: Watch out on your left!

WITH THIRTY YEARS OF MIDLIFE CRISES already, he drew a bead on the problem, known since the Greeks as Zeno's Riddle, where the turtle could only crawl halfway to the finish line. Since you could never measure a half with nothing on the other side, the turtle could never reach the end, and old farts were safe in the delusion they could try something new with all that time left to subdivide. And what with time being leaky, slippery, mostly spent conked out in front of TV reruns digesting a turkey pot pie, the second half always went faster than the first. Plus old guys were notoriously sloppy with instruments—channel changers, stop watches, ukuleles.

FOR HIM THE ONLY THING BETTER than making love was making love laughing, a rare and special gift that got no more common with the years. So much lovemaking seemed a counterfeit of pain, its appearance a grimace, its demands voracious, its earnestness a mask. Surely intimate moods could be endless. But the proof of joy was its release, laughter that outran its source, that built on itself like love did all the way to exhaustion. What could be better than the sleigh ride of the bodies raised to a raucous power? And who would dare call it delusion, this rollicking ecstasy where you were both in on the joke, and still got carried away?

AND BETWEEN THEM it didn't have to be a gut-wrenching laughter, an explosive gully-washer. It could be all-but silent—a joy beaming to bursting, a full moon rising out of the water, a laughter of wavelets drawn lapping to the shore.

IN A RAGE AGAINST ORDER perhaps sensing a chance for impromptu theater, some clowns were always on the muscle, rejecting lines and queues. On the freeway a bevy of cars all traveling the same speed was an invitation to elaborate stitchery, to weave out and in, or blowtorch through frozen sculpture. At the grocery checkout some clowns loved those Express Lanes with twelve items or less, and proved time and again who really counted. In the post office there was no hope, so they had to get out their cellphones and let one and all hear them bitch through the wait. Then when they got to the counter they'd hold a finger up to the clerk, still commanding Kazakhstan-Singapore-Bangalore to pile more chimps on a pin, saying Just a minute.

HE RECALLED ONE COUNTRY KID who said he smoked to stunt his growth. Country kids might crave to be jockeys, but most got too long and heavy for success. City kids mostly had no clue which side of a horse was up, so never knew the elation and terror of urging on the great beast made of blood and wind and desire, a thunder of hooves and bunched muscle, driving for the finish stretched out along its neck. It was a lesson to be learned, that we were all jockeys, that sometimes who you were was as nothing compared to the creature you rode, whether you were up on Traveler or Dan Patch, Exxon Mobil or the U.S. Senate.

FARMING ALWAYS HELPED HIM ease on down into fall. The harvest would arrive like bales of hay, all its work and worry compressed—then the payoff came, and then the well-earned rest. Things accelerated toward a close. The only other thing like that for him was baseball. The bat would sting your hands on chilly April nights under the lights, then again come late September. The games would slow, as one by one the teams would fall away. Who played this hard and this well with a wintry bite in the air, but the best of the best? Who played with that grand ease and poise and attention, who trusted themselves to prove the healthiest and luckiest, down to the end of the end? Nowadays the winners wore goggles to spray champagne on each other, but even that was old hat. Fall winners always squandered what was saved up once they'd answered with an out or walk-off home run the final inning.

BUT ALONG EDGES IN BACKWATERS and out in wide-open country, old ways were never done. Dirt farmers would make jokes about the new knife-sharpener their grown kids bought them, that you didn't need to find your glasses or a bright light for, just plugged in, that ate the blade down to nothing before you even thought to shout Slow down. Ruined all your knives before you caught on—the point wasn't to steal the whetstone business, but sell knives. Besides, some folks never knew or trusted a sharp one—just mashed down through their tomatoes, the messy old ripe kind.

THE OLD FARMER WAS LEARNING to dress for the occasion. And avoid ladders. The pears were almost ripe, but the tree was tall, and out of reach the pears refused to drop. So he put on a construction hardhat and went out to shake the tree. When they started coming down he hugged it, danced with it, and nearly every one missed him, didn't hurt or bruise a bit.

AGING FOR CLOWNS WAS MORE OF a ripening that just went on and on, never quite arrived at a soggy mess. Clowns were born weepy with blubber-lips anyhow, and pratfalls demanded lifelong practice, perfecting the whoopsie and look of blank surprise. Then there was throwing pies, that tended to drift off-target, flip in flight. Pies were a perfectionist art that only scored direct hits, like the high-dive bellyflop.

HIS OLD-GUY FACE SEEMED TO GET ever more serious even as his spirits lifted. It was a mug practically meant for spinning stories, telling jokes, that droopy deadpan delivery insisting he never got the point and never would, even when he sat down on it.

ON A NEIGHBORHOOD STROLL he came across a sloping stretch of lawn that held several hundred dinosaurs. The smallest of these Stegosauruses and Brontosauruses and Velociraptors and Triceratops were a couple inches long, while the largest, a Tyrannosaurus Rex, was lord of all he surveyed, a foot and a half tall sitting on his tail. This was no clash of armies, no Jurassic rock concert, no convention or parade, more like a migration all moving one direction, except for the king sitting down. It felt like they'd gotten a belated flood alert, and were on the march to Noah's Ark, trying not to stampede. Later after dinner in the waning light he recalled what he'd seen, snatched his camera and dashed up the street to take their picture. But the vast herd had moved on without a trace, leaving not so much as a paw-print. So carefully arranged, not one toppled over—had it been a grandparent's collection shared with a favorite child? But then where were the signs of mayhem that youth so enjoyed? Someone had been playing, but it was stately, purposeful. Had he caught an animated movie in the making, on its lunch break? But there were no chalk marks on the sidewalk, where a camera might have been set. No boxes of stunt doubles, no spare dinosaur parts off to one side, no empty coffee cups.

LIKE THEIR SMART DOG THE OLD CLOWN watched other creatures for clues. How some had long ago learned to live around man, let themselves be petted and fed, trained, even dominated made the best deal they could in trade for food, work, shelter and safety against the supreme predator. Animals that could outrun, outhunt, outswim, outpull and outfight naked humans had worked out a deal. Then there were wild ones who kept their distance, their edge and their smarts, who hid and flew high and harbored a timeless distrust. Among larger animals the numbers of both shy and aggressive ones kept dwindling. Then there was a third kind, maybe brightest of all, the ones who had learned to live around man and laugh at him, like crows, magpies and mockingbirds,

148

stealthy ones like raccoons, rats and possums, and newcomers possessed of a daring and arrogance like Canada geese and gray squirrels, who would loiter, beg handouts, even rummage through garbage to see what man had to offer, that he wouldn't share.

BUT THE BEST DOG STILL LIVED A DOG'S LIFE. It seemed they'd just figured how to get along as sled dog and mushers when she started to slow down, wise up. Not running so hard after sticks and balls, not probing so fiercely each tiny burrow, napping more with her head on his foot to keep connected. One thing she didn't like and sighed over, how much time she spent with one of the big ones waiting for the other to return. Still, a hide-and-seek treat or two, a stumbling walk where she logged invisible comings and goings, sniffed questions and peed answers same as always, what more did living require? To lift her head and come when she was called, to bark greeting and warning at every footstep and knock.

THE OLD CLOWN WAS HAVING ANT TROUBLE, a present from his dead sister. Not trouble exactly, they just followed him home and got into everything. Liked to swarm and kill smoke detectors. Promoted competitive overeating since they would not be denied that final slice of pie. But these days when he'd reach out to snuff another little life licking toothpaste in the sink, he'd feel himself pull back and look up, as if in the shadow of some looming giant, muttering fair is fair.

OUT DRIVING HIS ANCIENT RATTLETRAP he thought how silly cars had become. Back when cars were simple, if one let you down you rolled to a stop to baby it. Remember how the windshield wipers would drag and you'd go blind each time you climbed a hill? Nowadays cars with computer brains behaved like narcoleptics or insomniacs, would doze off and roll to a stop, or chirp awake in the middle of the night. If you had a showy car it said you were going from one secure enclave to another, or else to the car's home burrow, that was warm and snug enough to house a family of refugees, if they didn't mind having no windows and a giant overhead door. To think that in order to go anywhere you had to climb into a cocoon of steel and aluminum, rubber and plastic that weighed twenty times what you did, that made you deliberately insensitive, remote. And the more vulnerable or self-important you felt, the thicker the padding you bought, the higher on the throne you sat. Now they offered cars that drove and parked themselves, watched themselves back up on TV and hit their own brakes. Pretty soon those that could afford it would type in a list and send the car to the store.

THE OLD CLOWN SAW HOW TECHNOLOGY had gotten out of hand, how the new labor-saving and responsibility-evading wrinkles became their own excuse, how someone was already doing it by the time the decision-makers even knew it existed. And there was so much quiet money to be made, that the new tricks and treats got to script and play out their own scenarios. That first someone shot somebody down with a drone to prove it was even possible. Then all the clowns got to play with the new toy before they even told the boss about it, then he got to play before he told his boss, on up the ladder. So machines replaced people, made money and made trouble, made war and rained down death dealt by gamers, by remote control.

BACKING UP HIS COMPUTER FILES he got it frontwards and wrong. And for a while lost everything. Distracted never listened while the machine warned Do You Really Want to Do This? Like the backup beeps of a garbage truck. Because mostly what did it matter? With rare exceptions the precious in time turned worthless. So he paid good money for a pro with a headlamp to tunnel down after these very words while their dance moves meant anything. On the way to drop off the hard drive he recalled a sweet snatch of a poem that once blew out his car window into traffic, that he should not have been looking at. No-where to stop as he watched it in the rearview mirror, flip-flopping, run over and over, random as publishing, endlessly lifted and flung.

HE WAS STILL SKETCHY ABOUT even buying seedless grapes, much less GMO anything. Yet Kraft's "cheese food product" label final-ly got him buying real cheese. But there was the rub. If they didn't have to tell you what went in it why should they? They were always fabricat-ing new foodstuffs out of factory leftovers, pig squeals and potato peels, trying to sneak stuff in. They were so sure they knew what was good for you, that in the dark days to come this pseudo-food was going to save the world, that they should be greeted as prophets, rewarded as godlike inventors, preferably both. At least junk food junkies would never miss a fix. And the creators were sure their short-term profit-driven concoctions were going to be fine in the long run. Would sit right on the stomach, pass the bowel test. A supermarket pyramid of red ripe tomatoes hard as rocks—what could possibly go wrong? Genetic tech's well-paid mouth-pieces dismissed consumers with the tired parental line that they knew best, asserting only the public's right to ignorance.

EVEN SO THE OLD CLOWN DECIDED these days folks knew entirely too much. Mostly shot from the hip, never sweated their sources or fact-checked, were so positive their surety became an absolute. So now every time someone mentioned a cultural or political icon, famous or notorious, some other righteous clown would jump down the person's throat to set him straight, press him to swallow their personal truth like a sword that made his endless gut a sheath. And what had these flawed humans done beyond their brilliant, sometimes spotty work but break laws and get caught or not. They mostly joined other flawed humans who went barefoot to the bathroom just like Nixon, and peed on their own feet.

YET FOLKS HAD GROWN WEARY OF PLAYING the passive audience for showoffs, and now all at once pixels and fractals and splinters of lives caught on smart phones offered fresh relief. Showed and spoke their inconvenient truths. Thereby some wrongs were righted, at least wrongdoers armored and entitled were met with shame in public. And these little movies offered an informal check on courts and police, even on those raising chickens, pigs and cows in steel cages. After all, the anonymous many were solving the puzzle of who-did-what by netting lives on the fly, capturing tiny moments that might leave a body wronged and enraged, or forever empty and limp.

WHEN HE WAS YOUNGER THE OLD CLOWN was better at pigeonholing, keeping things separate, neatly parked in their slots—so he could go out and play tonight, and come the morning do a big serious dance. But now if he even knew that dance was in the offing, he could hardly eat or sleep the night before. When he'd look out, the horizon was too vast, there seemed precious little room for much else. Then he remembered how young clowns wore their hats pulled down, couldn't see ten steps ahead on the sidewalk. Maybe he just needed to dig out his big old hat, aim low, and make sure his feet landed right.

PLAYING MUSIC COULD BE LIKE COOKING with a partner. You tasted things as they came together, seasoned lightly to let the ingredients shine through, and trusted each other. Otherwise it was like cooking solo: I'll do my thing, then you do yours, then we'll roll leftovers up in a burrito. With hot young players music was more nakedly ego, my band or yours, which quickly led to who hauls equipment, who owns amps and a van, who does the talking onstage, who calls the tunes and makes the set list, down to who collects and doles out cash. Which was where you drew hard lines, between performer and listener, between onstage and backstage, between what's commanded, what's requested, and what's shared. Music for him was always more a conversation that began with easy greetings, few formalities, that you hoped to relax and get past, but didn't always. A game where everyone's a player. Making something for the porch and kitchen table, around the room chopping, stirring, a little sweet-tart something in the air.

HERE WERE THESE STIFF OLD HANDS on guitar and slide and mandolin, still not whispering Pull over, stop here. Warmed up first, then with fewer notes and chords maybe, played with room to spare. But whatever you do don't quit playing. Tunes from the car radio wafting into the back seat where the baby clown lay with street lights swooping over, big band jazz and pop, crooners and yodelers and mountain breakdowns to the Buick's rumble, grownups singing along to the crackly Hit Parade. The hands had long ago learned to surprise him with what they remembered of what he hardly knew he knew, from folks plunking in the parlor and those late-night backseat rambles, where they went wandering in the dark without his sayso, without even his eyes, that they stumbled on and fell in step with, soon went humming and thumping alongside. He'd start snatches that would some way finish themselves, noodle through a dark windy thicket clear to some kind of finale.

THE ROCKY ROAD WAS FROZEN HARD, while the line of hungry clowns limboed round the block. The clown had to admit he had ice-cream scooper's elbow. But then he also had shoveler's knuckles, tire-changer's shoulder, box-lifter's toes and altar-boy's knees. What was left of him to handle the tough stuff a scoop at a time? Clowns were not known for their patience, but pretty soon it would turn soupy enough even he could dish it out.

HE DREAMT OF EAGLES NESTING in his back yard, in the ailanthus tree. Eagles were making a come-back, might be considered a sign of luck nesting here, but this was ridiculous. It was a huge wicker basket with a massive limb growing through its handle—big enough to hold a VW Bug or a couple cords of firewood, filled with young eagles. They were a fluffy noisy brood full of outrage and need, their basket precarious. Their weight would shift it and one or another would tumble out, save itself with a claw or beak the last instant. The eagle parents had been hunting pets and stealing food off backyard barbecues to feed their brood, but they were skinny and exhausted and had to quit feeding the youngsters. They were patiently waiting nearby for the basket to empty, for the babies to spread their wings and discover who they were. But the kids hung on and made such a deafening racket they woke him.

THERE WAS FOG IN THE VALLEY when he heaved up then fell back. In a fog of his own he dozed and dreamt of other fogs he'd known, of misty invisibility, how it drifted and stuck. How people on the road burrowed through it, pressed into its cottony wall, how some even sped up, in denial of all they couldn't see, as if gripped by a lust for catastrophe. How fog snuck in and gathered itself, then stood still, like a place holding its breath. Unnoticed, a modest ghost. How it could appear in any season. How birds didn't care to fly in fog, content to wait out its passing. How he liked to walk in the fog a little ways, as long as he couldn't get run down or too badly lost, where he could cheat and look at his feet on the path for clues and test his courage. Like an experiment in being blind, to take a step then stop and listen for whoever else might be out here groping around.

AGAIN HE WAS UP EARLY tying his shoes for a walk in the fog while the sky paled. The few other dogs and dog walkers he met appeared startled, as if a steamship or iceberg loomed toward them. There were no birds flying, no squirrels skittering, no cars and no commerce. It was dreamy and dense, watching his feet float and stumble. The fog muffled sight and sound, obliterated homes and yards, and as the light came it thickened, till everything substantial fell away, till for a while fog summoned ghosts of ancient trees erect and fallen, drifts of tangled branches, a myriad needles and leaves. And more: beavers in their lodges, bears in their dens, ghosts of ten million moccasined first people drowsing in their camps, of twenty million buffalo huffing in the chill air, pawing frozen ground. Then the sun broke through, and he found himself four blocks from home, two crows on a wire laughing over him.

HE'D HEARD THE MANTRA OF YOUNG CLOWNS repeated forever—live fast, die young, and leave a pretty corpse. But by now having been through a whole poker deck of open-casket funerals, some of those exits notably garish, wasteful, trivial, he had to say he'd never seen a pretty corpse. Nice makeup on some, but what made young clowns beautiful wasn't blush and lip gloss over fine bone structure. A waxy perfection in the box was no substitute for juices just under the skin still pumping to the beat. As every clown secretly knew, when you fell down death said Stop, where life said Get up quick, lest the body forget what it was up to.

AS FOR BEAUTY IN ALL ITS GUISES, it could be an illusion confused with cosmetics, but also cause for wonder. It was mostly the province of youth, of the moment when life budded and bloomed, fruited then fell away, though some perfected its grace and allure into a lifelong dance. For some sad ones, beauty entailed a Charm School curriculum, where management of one's physical assets was the day's primary work. But generously dispersed without self-consciousness like a pollen in the wake of one's heartfelt investments, beauty could be a lifelong elixir that drew the world along, ever skipping and waltzing.

THE HEAD'S TURN TO FOLLOW THE VISION of loveliness in motion often met with disappointment over the long term, under the settled focus of a steady gaze. But who had that? Moreover, muscles dwindled, skin wrinkled, flesh sagged. Plus you got a stiff neck. The wonder was the candle in the jack-o-lantern in a shitstorm still stayed lit, shed light enough to flash its gap-toothed grin through an all-night pumpkin-bash.

MAYBE LIFE ITSELF WAS AN OLD LOVE in an endearingly imperfect guise. Fashioned of laugh lines and crows' feet, the patched and scarred body in its frayed mended clothing, with bold splashes of dinner caught proud on the bib, one with the sunset's grand art smeared on the blind painter's smock.

THESE DAYS WITH CHANGE UPON HIM, with summer winding down, how could he not also love fall and winter, the momentary riot of colors overhead then rustling underfoot, the cooling down to a shiver, the tree's severe scaffold with its living stripped away? How the snowdrifts simplified, dampened outcries, made a black and white dumbshow of death and hid the clutter?

OLD CLOWNS WOULD CONFIDE IN HIM, say "I'm just glad I won't live to see it," meaning one or another manmade catastrophe, global warming, rising seas, the demise of all other species but buzzards, cockroaches, and real estate speculators far inland gobbling up soon-to-be waterfront property. Then too there was the Second Coming in these Latter Days, with the corporate takeover of government, the collapse of social comity, the end of interest on savings and demise of micro-growth economics. But thus it had ever been, a long line of impending dooms reaching beyond the Black Death of the Middle Ages, The Anglo-Saxon Chronicle's pious fables, beyond the cedars of Lebanon felled to build a desert. He imagined the ancient fear of those towering dark silent lives, linked with a wicked delight at feeling their fall shake the earth. But back there somewhere too loomed the Nuclear Holocaust and its global winter. From the dawn of his own time the clown recalled the logic of Mutually Assured Destruction, that let no one sleep at night but the makers of bombs in the thrice-filtered air of their bunkers.

ONE RECENT WINTER A GAGGLE of young clowns unbolted a picnic bench from its slab and slid it way out on the lake, on thin ice a hundred yards from shore. Next morning when the sun rose the ice got rubbery, and the hapless maintenance crew studied how to retrieve it. They tried a surf casting rod to send a messenger and pulley with a big treble hook to snag the wood, contrived various ways to feed a bigger rope that might let them haul it ashore. They spent half the day sketching and scheming, tried every rig they could think of, till it sank out of sight in the sunshine.

HE SAVORED THE LITTLE WHEEL SHOW of tricked-out skateboards and BMX bikes. The riders' offhand moves were essential clownery. Not really transportation, they were for styling your way, trailblazing traffic, subverting dreary urban terrain by rashing, burning and sparking back to the jungle it was. Making it all new, transcending obstacles, mad-rush-caterwauling down ramps and walkways and stairs. Like graffiti artists they craved to reinvent an ugly and meaningless cityscape ruled by shopping and property values, where humans had no more legal standing than as sheep to be shorn, then scattered. It was a hard concrete and steel world to be met with elbows and knees. You couldn't quite skate crutches, though he'd seen it tried. But from the first they scouted and possessed empty swimming pools, culverts that held water only moments a year, freeway underpasses, bridge abutments, wheelchair ramps, parking garages. Here skateboarder and BMX rider rode the range as novel cowhands minus cows, trespassing on harsh environs, sketching sketchy improbable moves in each others' minds, to tag without leaving a mark behind them anywhere.

FOR A LOT OF PEOPLE THESE DAYS clowns were passe, old hat, the warmed-over doggy bag of what had been a full-meal deal. Maybe it was just e-fear of confrontation, of performance in all its mutations, of life in a thin made-up skin. Yet inside you always knew if and when you turned clownish, in undercover stubble or in the blue bag with radio and camera, badge and gun. Sure, clowndom had lost its esprit de corps, its bogus diner's club card, and never had a golden parachute. Yet though every style had its day and its half-life, he thought clowns were still universal and true as a hopeless load dumped on the mind, that infants all learned to walk with, tried hard to straddle, never sat down on.

FACIAL RECOGNITION SOFTWARE had gotten so good that clown makeup hardly worked as disguise any more. Some holdup artists, protesters,

and purveyors of genuine mayhem had taken to wearing presidential clown
masks. But then what became of clown makeup as a badge of identity, as
a question entertaining its answer? The shape of the face under paint was a
lie meant to be seen through, never mind raspberry lips, tearstained cheeks,
nose bulbous enough without florid fake honker. Once the gleeful slapstick
marauder just wanted a chance at an audience, hoped to give them what
they came for, a playful deception, a clown fishing in a bucket, who'd regret
if he hooked that piranha.

IN THE MIRROR THE OLD CLOWN began to see how some moments he was his clown parents, then his clown children, even some moments his clown baby self. How he lived on in them and them in him, time driven backwards and forwards like a saw blade that cut both ways, worrying a raggedy path through a life. Or maybe time was more like the tide, with him a clam or barnacle, how stuck in place for the first half-life it rushed in and covered him, taught him to be content drinking what passed through, sucking its nutrients, holding his breath. Now with the tide turned, running out and away from him the second half, he had to learn to dry out, breathe and spit. Either way filtering what came, always a little more and less than himself.

WAS THE CLOWN A COMMUNIST FOOL among fools who denied his own selfish desires, or was he all selfish desires with no sense of anyone out there beyond him? There was grand passion, there was the hunt with its stalking and frustrated scattershot, then there was the birdfeeder of love, admired by cats, plundered by squirrels, with all its feathered fliers on a shopping spree. Though birds took turns, the birdfeeder seemed to trivialize and domesticate all it sustained, made small free ephemeral lives available as decoration to the sightseeing heart. If you built and stocked it they would come, all the while ignoring you, even as you ignored them, depleted their habitat, what they fed on, where they nested and lived. Now nature lived on as a zoo, as museum diorama, as backdrop for the wellfed, where the caged exotic ones went quietly crazy and the small plain ones took care of business, while skinny clowns on the wing eluded capture, endlessly gabbled and jigged.

AT HIS AGE HE WAS TRYING TO KEEP FROM a lip-smacking bitterness. He listened to young know-it-alls and old people whose pronouncements were just as cocksure. It wasn't just government, religion and politics, their arrogant cracks dismissed climate change and gas prices, economic recovery and where the damn jobs went. And doom upon doom, the melting polar ice caps and vanishing honeybees. He felt the whole system had fooled him, big clowns with electronic tweezers legally picking little clowns' pockets. But then sometimes late at night he felt he was fooling himself, had lived all along with false hopes. Trudging downhill, he wondered why should life be any different than it was. Why shouldn't everybody jostle for advantage, why shouldn't winners grow bigger as they took more of everything, paid top dollar to get laws passed to fit their waistlines and appetites? There seemed no way out, no way to make things better, make things fair. Maybe he should smash his clock and mirror, cut up his credit cards and ID, and hit the road with pockets full of duct-tape and WD-40 for emergencies, footloose in his mismatched clothes.

PREDICTABILITY HAD MADE EARTH a friendly place. Publishers used to print the coming year's Farmer's Almanac without a crystal ball, and mostly be right not just about when to plant and harvest, but when to plan outdoor weddings, how much sand and salt, sandbags and snowplows to have on hand for winter. They did it right and for a while got better at it. They measured the snow pack in the mountains, counted hurricanes in the Caribbean, typhoons in the South Pacific, forest fires in the mountains, measured rainfall all over, logged the timing of monsoons, whale and bird migrations, the loopy dance steps of El Nino. Charted the antic dispositions of the Jet Stream and Gulf Stream. Considered where we'd been and allowed for momentum and drift, Kentucky windage. But now what could they do? Like a medieval bishop blame the plague on the sins of the poor, on God's anger, which was fathomless? Blame the unplanned unwelcome multitudes, while insisting that any fix would be bad for business interested only in short-term profits, quarterly balance sheets, while the carbon count steadily mounted past 400 parts per million.

THE OLD CLOWN FELT FOR A WORLD weathering the violence of global climate change. Furious and endless winter storms, high-water hurricanes, wind and hail and ice storms, tornadoes, mudslides, flash-floods. Scorching droughts that lasted years. And what else? Earth-quakes and tsunamis like the ones that shattered Port-au-Prince, the Andaman and Nicobar Islands, Fukushima. But what could be done? In the dead of night when dark thoughts troubled his rest, his first wish was for a future that built better, built stronger, without cavalier makeshift construction pretending the bottom line was not lives, but econom-ics. Not to build and live on coastal lowlands, on alluvial flood plains. Which was easy to say, hard to do. Mostly it was not even being said. But why bother building a school or town hall in Tornado Alley that could be blown away? He remembered what a sailing friend told him they did when typhoons hit Samoa. Everyone knew to head for high ground, hug the base of a tree, and pray to the Earth Mother.

HE INVITED OTHER CLOWNS TO GO to a hardware store and look at the hurricane anchors sold to tie down mobile homes. One screwed into the ground might hold a calm horse for a minute, but not an excitable team. As for climate change in a nutshell, the answers most-ly seemed to amount to treading lightly, shepherding natural resources, reducing carbon emissions—which scared bankers and businessmen enough to act dismissive, pretend insult or outrage while they chased fossil profits at the expense of most other forms of life.

SO WIDESPREAD DENIAL, DELUSION, and selfish resistance to change forced him to consider the end of the planet as a hospitable home, at least till Earth rid herself of this human nuisance, ground and tamped down the waste, got back to mindless tussles between ant and termite, kudzu and honeysuckle, got back to building topsoil, growing weeds. But how should a clown feel about it? Guilty or sorry, or scared enough to run and hide? Serious science said humans were to blame, and he could already see there would be no escaping the hard, bitter taste of their failure.

FEARS DROVE SOME CLOWNS WILD, gave them no breathing space and no rest. Fear of heights, of teetering and scrambling on the ledge, fear of tight places, of crawling deep into caves, fear of vast empty seas far from shore, of the watery depths. Fear of storms, of lightning and high winds and earthquakes, of the fragility of life itself, of death by fright. Of the mind's mush in its leaky box with tongue latch and jaw hinges sprung, dripping onto one's bare feet, right where one's wits might be essential in a crisis, with things to be done here and now, where in the slippery goop of second thoughts one needed to watch every step.

STILL, THE END-OF-THE-WORLD CLOWN crawled in off the ledge, stuck a finger down his throat to throw up the pills in the toilet and live on, in spite of how rancid life tasted. Sure, he blamed climate change, freak storms, corporate everything, poisonous fast food, bought and paid lobbyists, corporate congressmen who passed laws written by winners to punish losers like him, even CIA drone strikes on pizza delivery boys who got orders switched. It was all part of the same vast identity theft and credit default swap conspiracy. He heard they were cloning beanie babies on an inkjet using GMO soybeans and high fructose corn syrup. He splashed water on his face and faced the truth—if he wore makeup sobbing to bed, every morning meant a new pillowcase. Something had to give, he knew just like everyone he had to change his ways, there was no free pass even for a clown with a license to squeal. Sure, his nose was special, a built-in night-light noise maker, but what had that ever got him but a tax audit. He combed his real hair, told himself to shape up and swallow his pride, but then turning over a new leaf his first day found he was too shaky to shave.

BESIDES, WHAT COULD ONE CLOWN DO? There were no real jobs any more, no work making real things—only lip-flapping, noisemaking, performance art. He could join them—slap on a smile, don a paper hat and flip burgers. What about college? By now a scam to fleece both kids and their parents into depression and debt. Their much-vaunted Critical Thinking should address the obvious: how companies outsourced jobs, identities and self-worth, and imported products and profits. Said We don't do the people thing, like it was a silly waste, an insult to their intelligence. He couldn't even teach kids, they were still laying teachers off, while kids had to bring their own toilet paper and Sharpies in backpacks, along with a sandwich and some fruit, to be swapped on the lunchtime black market for something sweet to make them jabber, glow in the dark and climb walls. Yet nobody made their own coffee, that was beneath them, or washed windows or dishes or changed their own flat tires. There were homeless guys with cardboard signs on every off-ramp holding up traffic, begging for a buzz to keep the cold out, stalkers staring down anyone who could still scrape together a ride.

160

So he laced up his boots for the deep shit and decided, plainclothes clown it was.

ON SECOND THOUGHT, DROWSY THE CLOWN decided he'd take a rain check, flopped back in bed, pulled up the covers, tried to let go and drift off. He could see most of his life was hanging on, waiting for things to show up and threaten awhile till they got bored listening to his teeth chatter, and moved on to hunt someone else. Finally sleep took him away to dream he grew a long monkey tail, that let him swing in the treetops with his hands free to rain down rotten fruit. It was such a pleasure laughing out loud he woke himself.

AS THE PLANET GOT OVERCROWDED, poisoned, ground down, used up, the search was on for other worlds with some of the building blocks that made this one so sweet. Not precious gems and rare minerals, but a little dirt, air, water, not too cold or hot for animals and plants. The search began to feel like science and politics had surrendered, were willing to settle for escape from this failure, rather than work through delusions and night-sweats, human frauds and cons and lethal disagreements, to find earthbound solutions that might let the living sweetly carry on, without trampling or starving itself.

SENSING NO ALTERNATIVE, some sounded the planetary death knell. But was there truly no closing the widening social gulf, no walking the road back from deep-dish comfort and smug entitlement armed with a concealed carry permit? With fossil forces so entrenched was the only answer revolution? What about walking with knapsacks to spread and share the load? And what about governments that truly governed, decided and acted on matters with the people's consent, informed and vigilant, with none of this partisan nastiness? Otherwise the end would be no laughing matter, with denial and resistance to change willing to risk all life forms on this fragile blue-green planet, gambling on a sketchy status quo.

FEARFUL RIGHTEOUS HUMANS for thousands of years had paraded signs that read "Repent—the End is Near!" Now as he greeted returning birds he wondered which ones had he not even missed, wondered how they carried on amid small signs and wonders, with ends in sight everywhere. Fire sales had been an urgent ad gimmick until companies started announcing fire sales every few months, continuous fire sales in smoke-filled showrooms, shouted doom and despair as everyday business, until state officials laid down the law—only one fake fire sale a year.

CONSIDERING HOW FAR THE FUTURE stretched, how long the good might be forgotten and the bad be sung, what more could be done? Posterity wasn't like Jacob Morley wandering the night wearing chains, more like one of those movies where two criminals were chained together on the run. Proving how good and bad, fast and slow, old and young, even sworn enemies were practically identical, how circumstance or twist of fate could forge unbreakable links between the extremes found in most of us. Kids called everyone over 30 a sellout, a hypocrite, and no wonder. He watched old people try to clean up their act, edit their past, pretend their oblivious deafening young selves had never been. But good luck with that. Folks remembered not just how you wore your hair and changed your tune but what and who you had done. And everyone kept score—not just parents and children, siblings, classmates, erstwhile business partner cellmates, but people you'd never met who could still spit out your name. Memory forged links of hacksaw steel into an endless chain. Of course some acts were unforgivable, but most were reckless, ill-considered or plain dumb. So why not start with compromise, fair play, forgiveness—else we were all doomed.

ONE DAY HE WOKE WITH A START to the notion that life was pulling out of the station. Dozing in his seat for the moment he couldn't tell was he even faced forward or back. Everyone and everything he knew, all he had figured out and made connections with, was changing out from under him, heaving him from side to side as it went its own way, gathered speed. He sensed how precious little of the familiar would be left, and those not the parts he felt sure of. Even so he couldn't be talked out of such connections, such lifelong biases, though they felt harmless enough, like a taste for air and water and sunlight, a whiff of mint down by the river, a slice of melon or kumquat.

AND HE SAW THE TIME MIGHT COME when he'd get scared, turn obsessive and self-involved, worry about his prospects—where he'd sleep next, what he'd eat when the next hunger struck. Until then he could savor the passing show, present as if absent, walk to the store to buy grub to carry back, maybe poke some seeds in the dirt that would reach up, leaf out, feed him what they fed themselves. Which was the whole trick of farming, spying on what plants and animals fed their young. An apple or peach offered the seed its first good meal. He wasn't so good at weeding, which might be seen as random murder in a crowded world, though like brushing your teeth, you had to make time and just do it.

YET COULD HE BE PRESENT AS IF ABSENT, could humans walk with an airy feathery footprint? Could folks use less, waste less, unlearn ancient habits of greed and privilege, share not just thoughts and feelings but rides, meals and goals? It was hard enough for the child to learn to share his toys. In grownup economics, success meant never sharing toys, or anything else for that matter. You might want to burn it all down in a fit of pique once the novelty wore off, but you couldn't even take it with you when you went.

HE FOUND A RUSTY HORSESHOE NAIL in a city gutter a dozen miles from the nearest horse. Such trinkets did not grow on trees. Did it mean things were falling apart, for want of a nail and so forth, death to the whole barefoot army? Or was it a sign of hope, that horses had passed this way once and would again, when the oily nightmare was over, when the frenzied earth could take a slow breath, rest in the shade in a breeze? Horses were smart—they loved shade and water and new grass, fit in and knew right what to do with it, had no need to wear a shoe or turn a profit.

SOMETHING WAS BITING THE OLD CLOWN on the butt so bad he took his pants off, turned them inside out, turned the bright lights up and put his glasses on to check out every little thing. A wasp or spider, a thorn, a sliver of glass, a piece of guitar string, a splinter— something invisible he never did locate. With nothing else to do he spanked himself where it hurt and put his pants back on. And felt better. At least there was nothing and no one else to blame.

DAYS LIKE THIS HE FELT HE WAS LOSING the sharp edges of the world, in sight and sound, in touch and taste and smell, as his senses dulled and forsook him. Numb fingers, roaring ears, fuzzy eyes, snuffy nose, putty tongue. Balloons could still be made to pop by sheer persistence, but it seemed as if the world were retreating, even as he ached to rush out and take a fresh hold, one more time pull it close. Except for transcendent wonders at sunrise and sunset, this seemed all the dance he had left, based not on the mad dash of old, but on the dip and saunter and whoopsie.

THEN ONE DAY WALKING OUT OF THE BLUE lightning struck something behind him, the top of a power pole. Flung him to the ground, skinned his hands and knees. He wasn't hit by this stray bolt, this astonishment, it just deafened him, turned his brain to jelly, singed his halo, made him feel himself gently for damage. Left him calling his shaken self Lucky, as he coaxed the trembling three-legged dog of the spirit back to its feet, when all it craved was to dive in the bushes and howl.

HE WENT WINE-TASTING WITH FRIENDS in gold rush country southeast of Sacramento, but even drinking before noon couldn't make himself spit out the sips he took. Separating the taste from the effect seemed somehow foreign to the venture, pretending this was just a shopping spree. And lying there in a strange bed at night he recalled the supercolony of ants at his dead sister's house, that had hitchhiked home with him a thousand miles. How the ants had seemed endlessly curious about her, investigating every little thing, though they left his things strictly alone. Why? He suspected they knew he couldn't help but kill them wherever he fingered one, on table and counter, in the sink, set to deny them a taste of what he was cooking, since they flavored whatever they touched.

WINE WAS AN ESSENCE REFINED OF the place where grapes bloomed, a matter of soil, air, water, sunshine, leafy vines, of rooted living stirred by a breeze. Beyond the death of the year wines were fermented, conjured, compounded, from what had been mere juice and yeast, handfuls of skin, stems and seed. Winemakers could barrel and bottle only so much of this essence of place and time, and as each year was different, so too were its flavors. But wine-loving clowns knew to go to the fields on a light-hearted mission, openhanded in fair company, and there drink it down. Knowing back home it could never compare, though it might improve in memory, next to the real thing laid away in the dark on its side.

THE ART OF LIVING LONG ran afoul of the Law of Diminishing Returns. Farm fields needed to be manured and limed, crops rotated, land let lie fallow a season. A good rut was still a rut. So too as they aged clowns needed to waltz to new music, entertain new thoughts, try new tricks, play new games, deepen their studies and rest, search out renewal and change. Given exquisite footwork and timing, they still had to step to new tunes.

YET AGING IN SOLITUDE HE FINGERED discarded yesterdays. When he was young he recalled how quickly each day past was erased by new days piling on, how they merged and composted in the heap gone before, rarely turned up again, got his attention only as history— an overdue bill or pregnant memory that somehow insisted on itself. Sometimes the pile toppled over and decades got shoveled aside. But lately his days passed without fanfare but for the overheated news of a wicked world kept at armslength. It didn't much help that he'd cook a pot of beans and rice with an onion, bay leaf and ham hock, to eat till it was gone. And he didn't read so many books cover to cover, spent more time surveying modest swindles like cough drops, dripless underwear, skinless franks.

LOOKING INTO THE MIRROR NOW he mostly just waved back at that organism rooted in space and time, how it peered out at the world. That could still feed itself, draw nourishment where it stood, could bend to rushing winds and waters that swept past. He could see stubbornness in the glass, but no refusal to change, no easy letting go. No demand to be treated certain ways or else. The lights were still on back in there somewhere.

THE TIME ARRIVED WHEN HE DIDN'T SET an alarm anymore, since why bother. He never slept all night, no more than several hours at a stretch. Unless he'd lost a night somewhere, forced the machine to crash-land or pull over. He'd get up to go pee, then might snatch up a book or notebook to relieve that other overactive organ, so it would let him drift off. So mostly time lurched and snuck up on him, and early or late when he woke there it was.

SOME DAYS HE FELT THE WEIGHT of his years, when no aria sprang unbidden to his lips, no jaunty pronouncement of the obvious. Time was running out—one more spring, one more fall, the seasons seemed to roar through him, made him gush and choke like a storm drain clogged with leaves. His hands felt stiff and outsized, even in warm weather catchers' mitts hardly up to carrying a tune, much less tickling the guitar. It all ran down, like maybe this one life was just a rocky narrows in a river, where the pace quickened, where burbled manic nonsense hardly held the makings of a song as it passed on, spilled into the one ocean that always had plenty of room.

WHAT WOKE HIM AGAIN AND AGAIN through the longest night of the year, to savor the rain slashing windowpanes, rinsing the dark neighborhood? Maybe it was like nights on the boat, when he sat up to check his position, see if he'd drug anchor. He stood to see up and out through the town's glowing dome, to find the few lights scattered overhead. Some were planets that offered steady faint twinges of color, reflected like the moon and earth itself, and some were sparkling faintly pulsing suns, their lights rippling on invisible currents spanning the fathomless depths. And nearby, passing through, space junk and satellites. For the moment in all that rainy blurry waste, nothing appeared out of place.

AT THE PASSING OF PHIL EVERLY he savored the high spare art of harmony. How the singers had to be listening and responding, not competing, each holding back part of himself, tuned to a common goal. And as Phil and Don said of their shared inflection, Pronounced the same words the same way. How the club of great practitioners was small, but included some memorable songwriter-performers, like Lennon and McCartney, Simon and Garfunkel, Linda Ronstadt and nearly anyone she chose. How the songs of loneliness and lost love performed with such harmonies cut through background noise in a way nothing else could, made the listener even in his loneliness feel joined and whole. Their singing brought to mind twin fiddles, Astaire and Rogers swooping up and down stairs, ice skating couples, barn swallows feeding at twilight on the wing in pairs.

PETE SEEGER HAD JUST DIED, and he got out the banjo to ponder that label stuck on him, "folk singer." Unelectrified one-man-music-maker, Pete could suck in anyone who had a heart and lungs to sing along. There would always be music that was one performer or group showing off, displaying their coordination and unity of feeling, their fancy licks that hushed the crowd to watch. But Pete never wanted that, his music an engine of change, a tall order borrowed and cobbled together, focused and clarified, a soulful declaration sung straight out and up, soaring aloft till all in his presence felt lifted.

HOW TO LIVE WITH ONE'S DEATH in the forefront of the mind, looking out the bleared windshield at what was rushing toward him, what he was rushing onto without brakes? Waved at in passing, other lives invited comparison. Plants, their sloughing off and greening on, their flowers and swelling fruits. Insects that inspected and tasted each bit of the living, whether they swarmed the air, tunneled dirt and wood, or foraged overland. Furred and feathered lives reaching up beyond his ken or beneath him burrowing, that appeared to proceed without crippling self-consciousness or fear. That went their ways in cycles of youth and fruition and decay, that migrated or stood fixed in an eternal here-and-now. Some seemed capable of memory and desire, but all embodied what they knew, wore their scars and years, indifferent whether their meaning be read aright or mistranslated, or taken for the illiterate scribble of winter storms upon a once-smooth skin.

COULD YOU BITE DEATH and not have it bite you right back? Only with suicide, where you cheated death's approach, which also cheated you of watching life depart, the wink and wave that was unique and one to a customer. All that living poured into the cauldron, awaiting the final stir. Who knew what the synapses might register, what rhythms and flavors they'd conjure in those final leaps and sparks? What green flash bobbed the ocean to the west? Fear of pain in the end seemed a cheap excuse. Frank Sinatra sang I Did It My Way thirty years, but that was self-delusion or theater—never past tense till the stage lights went down and the house lights came up as this sleepy little hamlet emptied out into the night.

THERE WAS SOMETHING TO BE SAID for wind-up chattering teeth, but what? No lips no tongue no words no bad breath. It was like what the movie star hoped for, the writer, the poet—an immodest immortality, a form of life after death. At least life after the last tooth dropped. The smiling essence of politics, the full set of teeth that signaled I could bite you but won't. But what did the wind-up teeth ever really say but Wind me up and turn loose of me? They wanted to keep talking, like a bad performer at an open-mike. They wound down chattering on, refusing to look at the clock. Taking up everyone's time, who cared what they clattered about.

HE WAS CONSIDERING PREMONITIONS, ends and beginnings. How at 15 you caught a glimpse of the grownup you might become, what thoughts and worries might possess you, what works and games of a life aswarm with complications—endless choices, chance collisions, close calls. How this breathless act of imagination would stagger the young clown, tuck him back into hiding for another half-dozen years. Now on that other verge, he felt an ache unravel the bones of his spine, that might signal dissolution or be knit up by a nap and a couple pills. Then acting out an oblivious classic, crossing the street against the light he was snatched by a dizzy spell, forced to plop down on the curb and catch his breath. Such times panting he wondered, Is this the beginning of the end, the path he'd stumble down? But then he shook off the specter, and mounted the delusion like a unicycle that let him wobble along, hitching, backing and filling, immortal as they come.

HE CAUGHT A LESSON FROM THE TALENTED hardworking Olympic gymnasts: you don't get to stick the dismount. He'd seen too many go down hard, and a rare few go down easy. Sure, there were drugs, and sure, you could get lucky, with luck the residue of endless preparation, as some great coach once put it. But the stumble-step landing in a headlong spiral off the beam or rings or uneven parallel bars was a tipoff, that this would take not just all your practice, but art and luck, so was like living at its height, that rare, not like living at its finale. What such an electric display was most like was putting the magic sword back in the stone where it might rest another thousand years, till the next one gave a yank with sufficient grip and strength.

HIGH IN THE STANDS under buggy floodlights he watched rodeo clowns helping bull riders once they were thrown. Helping all comers, mostly losers, but now and then a champion. Because, unless quickly distracted, bulls would butt or hook a cowboy, stomp him into ghost pizza. He hung around the dressing rooms under the grandstand afterward, watched them clean off their grease paint, saw smiley faces wiped away, loud baggy pants set aside. They reminded him of Seabees from the war in the Pacific, jaunty building landing strips and loading docks under fire, their work slapdash but for the moment indispensible. He tagged along to the Nugget Bar, where without makeup and fright wigs they were hard to keep track of—like firefighters on a night out, the young ones looking for action, the old ones looking to unwind.

THE DRY OLD CLOWN REGARDED his sagging creased face puttied over, his drooping jowls and ears and chin. His blind excitable tongue footloose in its gaping pie-hole, his big red lips and deep frown amplified to uncork outsized passions. His flexible flippers unhinged to paddle through doldrums. The pearl of a tear from his misting eyes that dripped off his nose, that he wiped away with a thumb. The blubbering he couldn't help that kept up like a dog left alone in the dark, barks and whines that meant no more than he did, that just wanted a sofa to chew on, if he couldn't have someone to sleep beside, someone playful and warm.

HE USED TO BE MOVED ON THE WATER. Sailing meant life to him, sometimes a waiting game, mostly a fair bargain struck to make his way, negotiating wind and waves, and subtle powers-that-be. Then for years he'd felt stuck, anchored in current, not moving with it, much less with the wind, his anchor fouled on something far below he couldn't lift. He remembered catching a sunken car once, how the tug that pulled him loose pretzeled his hook. Another time with his anchor caught on logging junk in deep water he had tried everything, even risked a rising tide sinking him, but finally cut his anchor line to free himself, and felt something lift and rejoice.

TO THE AILING CLOWN LIFE BEGAN to seem porous, diaphanous, his body like a leaky wooden boat half-sunk with rain in the shallows, drinking in the past. Pressed against a mud bottom, he could only hope his seams would swell shut in time to be refloated, and bob again, buoyant.

OLD CLOWNS FORGOT IF they'd even been here before. Lounging through reruns in their lazyboy recliners, where only pieces and snatches lit up. Their catnaps blurry snapshots out the windows of a moving train. Yet there was comfort in the notion that every dawn arrived freshly painted, an original. And every sunset broke the mold, no way one ever repeated. And mostly these days they got to see both, the set clearly matching or mismatched, then in-between let the body fidget till it found a rest-stop, called a halt.

OLD AGE ARRIVED THESE DAYS LIKE WINTER, a bright breathless morning once in a while. He could be mesmerized by a shape-shifting snowfall, its drifts and erasures, its solemn burials. How it mounted fence posts, made trees bow, saved things dropped in passing for later. Then it was back to the chill and bluster, trees stripped to skeletons waving shredded banners, a wet sloppy misery, or test of the stoical, stiff and bone-dry.

EASY, HE SAID TO THE BODY, the one in pain. Lie back down. Though this time it had been weeks since he'd stayed up all day, he was trying to see through the fog, ice crystals floating in low light that seemed to shiver up out of the ground. With pain it was always now, never later, never conditional if or when. He was trying to whisper lest he call attention to himself, to the pain that sat astride him, that seemed intent to ride him down. He was only trying to slither into his socks, then stagger-step into his loafers, then heave himself back up into his life, a feat that today seemed beyond him.

in the afterglow

"…But since that I
Must die at last, 'tis best
To use my self in jest,
Thus by feign'd deaths to die." –John Donne

HE DREAMT HE WAS STANDING at the entrance to the big top, with the sun going down, the lights coming on, outlining the tent's graceful curves, together both sails and boat. Somewhere an organ was playing. Inside there was a hubbub as the audience settled in, a mounting susurration as of cicadas and bees. But the entertainers weren't quite ready. They were still scattered around the field, playing, picnicking. A few rehearsed routines they were about to perform, pacing out miniature steps, lifting, turning. Twirling aloft their juggling clubs. Silently he waved for the clowns. Reaching high overhead, his hand felt like a giant catcher's mitt that took an effort to lift and swing. But the clowns turned to it like a beacon, and rose as one to come in.

THE BULLS WERE WILD THROWBACKS bred with no hint of nurture, pure muscle and attitude, easily enraged. And the matadors were no mountain men to wrestle their horned malice barehanded to the earth. They were slight, steely and swift, ornately dressed, could bend without breaking, could stand their shaken ground as the bull driven to distraction stabbed at them and missed. In the arena, conducted with skill and dignity, there was nothing clownish to this dance of death. The plot of each story the same, with once in a while a reversal, the one bafflement why any culture demanded such an ancient spectacle, that insisted on death as its finish. Only outside running the bulls through the streets did some clowns itch to toss their lives into the air like fresh-cut flowers.

THE DEATH RIDE WASN'T THE ONLY amusement park ride, surely didn't entertain long with its abrupt turns from thrilling to lethal, but seemed like the one ride that stuck. Its burrs under the saddle made the

171

mind circle back while the ride was slowing down, to watch what reached out, nibbled at it like a wheel of fortune ratcheting toward a stop. Since the dawn of human time, since the lights went on anyhow, people had been asking Now what. Not so much where did we come from, which was an endless slow-motion train pulling out of a dark station mostly barefoot, but where were we going now, which was only the cry of the child after a long day overfed, over-excited, over-tired, while it was still light out refusing to be tucked in, told to rest.

HE DREAMT HE KEPT THE SUNKEN BOAT tied to the dock for a Viking funeral. In his dream the thing was wood, screwed, glued and caulked the old way, seams worked to weeping by a life in heavy seas, by battered living in motion. As for the dying, the boat was caught and stuck, sails torn free, could not be refloated, nor set afire in a show of mock dignity. So its finish would be slow—worn down by inertia, indifference, neglect, ratcheting and grinding past a halt, dead engine choked by sand and silt, the floater grounded, its hull violated, splinters now awash, lifted and flung up the beach over stones by the incoming tide. Where expired now frayed beneath itself it would be drug up and down, scoured until its very notion moldered—till the slightest particle recognizable as boat wandered off, unbound, released.

FUNERALS WERE FOR THE SOLACE and repair of those left hanging on, survivor clowns on ice floes comfortably numb. Some used them to keep score, though spelling and counting were optional. Funeral clowns never bothered saying hello or goodbye, started in right where they left off years before. They saw both greeting and leave-taking as a waste of time, since either you were here or you weren't. In the end the farewells caught up with you, which is why funerals all ended early or ran late. Sometimes the funeral turned out to be about the one you found you never knew until released from life without parole. That you'd been holding out on, that you suddenly unaccountably missed. That you'd have welcomed if they had come. That might be here right this minute, unrecognizable in the funny suit and hat, it's been so long.

BUT WHO NEEDED TO GET DRESSED UP and go out only to be reminded he used to be someone but was now a nonentity. Once wore a hat full of fat sparks that might have set off serious fireworks, at least hid a bad haircut, kept the dirt out of his eyes while he fooled with the plumbing and wiring. Now his clothes looked too big on him anyhow, and he'd rather be back in pajamas with his trainwreck feet propped up, waiting for some silly snack to arrive and some silent movie to come on, soon as the sunset pulled those burning spears out of his eyes and let him see.

THE OLD CLOWN KNEW HE WAS DYING, no fooling. Every day he appeared more clownish, ragged, inept. Didn't need any more makeup, why bother—owned the frown he worked, why paint one on, or the eyebrows' twin peaks of astonishment. When asked for a urine sample, he pulled his old gag of filling it with apple juice when the nurse wasn't looking, so when she came back he could hold it up to the light, say It looks a little cloudy, think I'll run it through again, pop the lid and chug it. For a while there every little thing he said or did seemed worth a laugh, though his face felt frozen, his cheeks sagged to his knees by the weight of the life he had swallowed. That last day when they asked what he wanted, he couldn't decide between jello and a milkshake, so they brought him both. And while both sat by his elbow and melted, sweated rings into the nightstand, he dozed his final minutes off and on, waking just in time for the finale. In the light failing as it reached for him he heard ducks and chickens feeding, that might have only been the nurse's brand-new shoes.

author's note

Not all clowns were infantile show-offs, loud and frightening. Some were silent, fearful and shy, worked to fit in, get along, divert attention from themselves. Still, his mutterings and arias, his snuffling in the dirt and scenting of the night wind, his pregnant lapses and blurted wakenings bespoke insights mostly fleeting, momentary. The candle guttered, the night surged over him. So these pieces landed like leaves from the tree all a jumble, though the intention was soon plain: the autobiography of an innocent in prose poetry.

As for shape, though living is sequential, it is often not consequential. It is understood and savored in loops, in dreams, in recovering ground often long thought lost to feeling. So pieces were posted on social media over a couple of years, one at a time in no particular order, to see if the form would catch at the sleeve of the passerby, see what took. And to see if, appearing cut from the life with a tin snips, these parts could be sung in tune anyhow, in outlandish harmony.

Yet it seemed to take forever to shut the lid on the work. It was like a bulging clown suitcase with defective latches, that kept popping open at the least excuse—so proofreading or polishing, even going to throw out something might still mean a gain in weight. Pretty soon in clown style it felt like it needed a stout friend to sit on it while he took a shears to anything left hanging out. Sure, there were gaps to the story, but these were decorative chinks like the grillwork in the Alhambra to cool the hot days within yet keep private, chinks that could be filled or let be, seen through not as imperfections but as airing for the mind of the poor reader short of time and breathing room.

A native of Ohio and Indiana, PAUL HUNTER lives in Seattle, where he has raised two sterling children and filled the years with various strenuous pursuits, including teaching at the University of Washington and The Overlake School, driving bus for Metro Transit, rebuilding several engines on his kitchen table, making guitars, and most recently exploring and writing about sustainable small-scale farming. For the past twenty-two years he has published handset letterpress books and broadsides under the imprint of Wood Works. His farming poems have been reviewed in the New York Times, and have received the Washington State Book Award. He has been a featured poet on The News Hour. His boat Rockfish is still tied up ten minutes west of his home.

CPSIA information can be obtained
at www.ICGtesting.com
Printed in the USA
FSOW03n2304110217
30616FS